*ening to Grief*

"*Opening to Grief* is a wise and gentle companion, a refuge as we move through the pain of loss. We learn to honor and cherish what has passed and to embrace our living moments ever more deeply."

—Tara Brach, author of *Radical Acceptance* and *Radical Compassion*

"*Opening to Grief* invites readers to approach and be with their grief, rather than turn away and try to avoid it. The authors mix reflections with simple yet profound practices anchored in mindfulness. It's easy to read and a wonderful addition to the grief literature."

—Sue Morris, PsyD, director of bereavement services at Dana-Farber Cancer Institute, Boston, MA

"A wise and sensitive book, this guide to working with grief is a treasure."

—Joan Halifax, abbot, Upaya Zen Center and author of *Standing at the Edge* and *Being with Dying*

"*Opening to Grief* is as excellent, simple, and clear as a needed glass of water in the desert. I cannot think of a better companion for our current time of losses, named and unnamable. This trustworthy and poetically written handbook of solid, helpful practices is a wonderful guide to the landscape of grief and the rites of passage of mourning. Without ever suggesting that grief is something to 'get over,' it points the way to the reconstitution of identity that can follow a great loss. May it help you grieve with an open, rather than closed, heart."

—Katy Butler, *New York Times* bestselling author of
Knocking on Heaven's Door and *The Art of Dying Well*

"Reading *Opening to Grief* is like sitting with a wise friend who has walked the difficult road of sorrow ahead of you. Full of gentle and nourishing practices, this kind book offers a supportive hand when the ground beneath you has been shaken by loss. Listen to these two experienced travelers in the land of grief, and you will find your way through the darkest of nights. A beautiful gift to all."

—Francis Weller, author of *The Wild Edge of Sorrow*

"A clear, concise, and tender companion book . . . Having facilitated thousands of support groups, including ones centered on bereavement, I appreciate the emphasis on not trying to shoulder the burden entirely by oneself. The authors gently encourage the reader to accept and fully experience their grief, which ultimately will lead to new discoveries, greater compassion, and a deeper understanding and appreciation for life. Included are many helpful suggestions and guidance on turning to art, nature, meditation, and writing to aid in the process."

—Bob David, manager, cancer support programs,
Boston Medical Center, Boston, MA

"In a world of increasing isolation and deep sorrow, *Opening to Grief* offers the medicine needed: a companion of voices, deep reflection, and masterful guidance."

—Koshin Paley Ellison, cofounder of the
New York Zen Center for Contemplative Care
and coeditor of *Awake at the Bedside*

"This simple and powerful book is an invitation to let the light of awareness touch, love, and heal our deepest and most impossible sorrows. In this warm and supportive guidebook, the authors lead us through practices that tend to our broken hearts and illuminate the unseen places where we keep grief locked away."

—Will Kabat-Zinn, mindfulness and meditation teacher,
member of Spirit Rock Meditation Center teacher's council

"*Opening to Grief* affirms that expression and self-compassion in grief are soothing to the soul and that allowing our feelings to simply be is the most helpful way to move through and integrate them, no matter how painful. In this lovely book, Claire Willis and Marnie Crawford Samuelson invite the bereaved to meet grief with compassion and intention, and lovingly show the way."

—Karla Helbert, author of *Finding Your Own Way to Grieve*
and *Yoga for Grief and Loss*

"Any time we make a change, there's grief on some level. Leaving a job, a relationship—even a toxic one—can be painful. Losing a beloved companion can be insufferable. With the support of a spiritual friend or the guidance of a book like *Opening to Grief*, we can learn to be mindful in the midst of it all. And eventually, when we stand up after all we've been through, we can see the beauty of it all."

— Spring Washam, author of *A Fierce Heart*

"*Opening to Grief* is a simple and profound book for all who grieve. The authors are sure-footed, trustworthy guides on this complicated journey, and they lead with loving-kindness. This small book brims over with compassion, mindfulness, gentle guidance, permission, and well-chosen poetry to enhance the lessons of each chapter. A helpful appendix lists the often-asked questions about grief with respectful and accessible answers. I will have more than one lending copy on my office bookshelves."

—Kathleen Adams, psychotherapist, founder and director of The Center for Journal Therapy

"*Opening to Grief* is a gift to anyone who is bereaved. With beautiful language, comforting thoughts, useful suggestions, and accessible practices, Willis and Crawford Samuelson bring healing and community."

—Hester Hill Schnipper, LICSW, OSW-C, manager, Oncology Social Work, BIDMC, emeritus, author of *After Breast Cancer*

"*Opening to Grief* is a little treasure that invites us to read a chapter at a time, little by little, allowing the blank pages to remind us to give space to whatever we may be experiencing and to pause a minute before passing to the next chapter, as tempting as it may be. Beautifully written, *Opening to Grief* is a jewel waiting to be discovered."

—Brita Gill-Austern, Philip Guiles Professor of Psychology and Pastoral Theology, emerita

"*Opening to Grief* is a treasure—a book destined to support and inspire anyone living with grief, whether recent or from the past. The authors, skillful and experienced guides in lighting the way through grief, have assembled a sensitive, caring approach to one of life's greatest challenges. Written as a companion for handling grief, the poems, meditation guidelines, and many creative suggestions contribute to making this a reassuring, beautiful, and heartwarming book."

—Olivia Ames Hoblitzelle, author of *Aging with Wisdom* and *Ten Thousand Joys and Ten Thousand Sorrows*

"Never have I seen this much useful information about grief presented in such a clear and inviting way, in so few pages. *Opening to Grief* is carefully and exquisitely structured to include grief education, easy to understand meditation techniques, simple actions, inspiring poems and quotes, and blank pages for personal writings. Generously filled with resources, it's a practical book of wisdom that I will recommend above all others."

—Connie Baxter, bereavement program coordinator, Brattleboro (Vermont) Area Hospice

Opening to Grief

finding your way from loss to peace

CLAIRE B. WILLIS
MARNIE CRAWFORD SAMUELSON
Foreword by Megan Devine

DHARMA SPRING

This edition first published in 2022 by Dharma Spring, an imprint of
Red Wheel/Weiser, LLC
With offices at:
65 Parker Street, Suite 7
Newburyport, MA 01950
www.redwheelweiser.com

ISBN: 978-1-59003-526-9

Library of Congress Cataloging-in-Publication Data available upon request

Cover and text design by Kathryn Sky-Peck
Cover photograph "Boulder, Colorado, 2015" © Michael Wood
Typeset in Weiss

Printed in the United States of America
IBI

10 9 8 7 6 5 4 3 2 1

For all of you who have entrusted me with your grief,
I am truly grateful.

—Claire Willis

In memory of my mother, Marion Crawford Samuelson,
and my friend and coach Joseph Abbott.

—Marnie Crawford Samuelson

Contents

Foreword

For far too long, we've treated grief as a problem to be solved. Our spiritual teachings around grief lean heavily on transformation and overcoming the "darker emotions" (a phrase with deeply racist connotations). Our movies and books all stress the happy ending, and pop psychology (and pop spirituality) suggests gratitude as the cure for grief. Even books that seem good on the surface can have a subtext of correction or shame: "Do all this stuff we suggest and your grief should be cured. Don't feel better yet? You're not trying hard enough."

Things are changing. Saner, kinder, more inclusive descriptions of grief emerge every day. In *Opening to Grief*, Claire B. Willis and Marnie Crawford Samuelson's commitment to the normalcy of grief—and what it means to be human—doesn't falter. They won't tell you you're doing it wrong. They won't push you to move faster, work harder, let it go. What they will do is offer you the comfort of being seen inside your discomfort.

That's what's special about this book; it offers a way to engage with grief that doesn't seek to remove or erase it at all but help you meet loss on its own terms. *Opening to Grief* acknowledges grief as a sign of deep love, rather than a problem to be solved.

Willis and Samuelson offer practices to help you withstand and survive that which is directly in your path, immovable and unavoidable.

The work is not to remain unbroken by love and grief but to remain there, in the great brokenness, with your eyes and your heart open, refusing to look away. There is no need to transcend being human. Liberation is to be found in listening to yourself deeply and with kindness, extending that same respect to all beings. The road to a more just and equitable world begins with listening to pain.

May this book, and the practices herein, be your companion in the new world arriving every day.

—Megan Devine, author of *It's OK That You're Not OK: Meeting Grief and Loss in a Culture That Doesn't Understand*

Note from the Authors

On the last day of the world,
I would want to plant a tree.

—W. S. MERWIN

We wrote this book at a simpler time. At least it seemed that way. When 2020 began, our routines felt familiar, well within what we thought of as "normal." And we felt a relative sense of security.

Then the pandemic struck like a storm out of the Bible, a plague beyond what we could have imagined. We were working with our editor at Red Wheel/Weiser, to finalize this book about grief, describing Claire's life work with the bereaved. We wrote for people grieving personal losses, for example, the death of a loved one, such as a child or spouse or beloved pet, or the loss of a job, or the onset of a life-threatening illness. And then the world turned on a dime, and suddenly governments worldwide were mandating lockdowns, and we were all sheltering in place.

Where we live in Boston, April and May brought a surge of COVID-19 infections and deaths. An email Marnie received during the shutdown began: "I am writing with a heavy heart to tell you. . . ." It was about a friend from her meditation group who had been hospitalized and then died a few days later from the virus. That week, there were almost no non-COVID-19 stories in the news, as the U.S. pandemic death toll surpassed 100,000.

In a column in the *New York Times*, David Brooks asked readers how they were holding up during challenging times. In the first few days, he received 5,000 replies. "I think I . . . expected a lot of cheerful coming-together stories," Brooks told NPR. "But what I got shocked me. It was heart rending and gutting frankly. People are crying a lot . . . It tends to be the young who feel hopeless, who feel their plans for the future have suffered this devastating setback, a loss of purpose, a loss of hope. Then the old, especially widows and widowers, talk about the precariousness of it, the loneliness of it. They just feel vulnerable, extremely vulnerable. While a lot of people are doing pretty well, there's just this *river of woe* out there that really has shocked me and humbled me."

Now we see that aspects and qualities of grief and grieving are universal, whether you have suffered an individual loss, or are experiencing losses on a global scale. Individually and collectively, we are *grieving*. We're experiencing large, difficult feelings, even if we don't recognize them as grief: sorrow, fear, anger, anxiety, depression, hopelessness, or disorientation. These troubling emotions, sensations, and mind states are the ways we humans respond to loss.

We feel the loss of family members, friends, and neighbors we loved, celebrities and public figures we followed. We're missing the person we were and the way we lived not long ago. In the midst of this invisible, highly contagious virus, we grieve the loss of a kind of innocence. As we don our masks and gloves, we fear being infected or infecting others, and wonder what impact these changes will have on our worldview and our emotional well-being.

We grieve the loss of our work and economic stability, the familiarity of seeing our kids go off to school, and the ease of chatting with friends and even strangers. We grieve for shuttered offices, factories, and gathering places. We grieve for elders in nursing homes, family members who cannot visit one another.

In the midst of national protests over police brutality and systemic racism, we bear witness to the deep grief of the African-American community and other communities of color who also suffer a disproportionate share of deaths and infection in the pandemic. We grieve and are heartsick for families who have lost loved ones to violence. We grieve for the houseless and under-resourced, for children who are hungry, for all whose lives are sorely affected in these times.

We grieve graduations cancelled and weddings postponed. We're grateful for online memorials, friends and family get-togethers, and virtual religious services. Yet, we miss human touch.

We now know that the unimaginable can and does happen. And we've learned how deeply reliant we are on each other—how radically interconnected we are. We breathe the same air and suffer the same diseases. We're all in this together. We have witnessed the "helpers," as Fred Rogers called them, acting with selflessness and courage. We've seen the generosity and kindness of medical professionals, grocery workers, mail carriers, and delivery folks, the millions of *essential workers* who have kept us fed and alive.

We've seen how grief and love are intertwined. We grieve because we love. And we transform suffering and get through adversity by loving and helping each other. As we find ways to stay present, do what is right, persist against odds, we become like the poet W. S. Merwin and choose to "plant a tree" no matter what.

—May 2020

part one

Opening to Grief

THE THING IS

to love life, to love it even
when you have no stomach for it
and everything you've held dear
crumbles like burnt paper in your hands,
your throat filled with the silt of it.
When grief sits with you, its tropical heat
thickening the air, heavy as water
more fit for gills than lungs;
when grief weights you like your own flesh
only more of it, an obesity of grief,
you think, How can a body withstand this?
Then you hold life like a face
between your palms, a plain face,
no charming smile, no violet eyes,
and you say, yes, I will take you
I will love you, again.

—Ellen Bass

An Invitation

In the terrible days and months after losing someone or something dear to us, we may experience a swirl of painful emotions, moods, and even symptoms and sensations. Being in grief's terrain can be unspeakably difficult, a time when we feel lost, disoriented, brokenhearted, and unsure if we'll ever feel joyful or even okay again.

We have written *Opening to Grief* as a companion or guide for people who may be grieving deeply for the first time as well as for those who have lived with grief for many years. It is also a book for all of us who continue to bump up against cultural assumptions of "appropriate" ways to grieve.

As coauthors, we draw on Claire's decades-long work leading bereavement groups, listening as people sit together, courageously ask difficult questions, cry, laugh, and support each other in learning to bear sorrow and go on. Claire is also an experienced yoga teacher and Buddhist chaplain. In this book, when we use the pronoun "I," we are referring to Claire's life and work experiences. We also draw on Marnie's years as a writer, photographer, and storyteller; she is the primary wordsmith for the book.

Both of us practice meditation. We will introduce you to some basic ideas about being mindful: paying a kind of warmhearted attention to life as it unfolds in the present moment; being aware of your thoughts and feelings without getting caught up in them or judging them; relaxing and settling into calm and stillness; and feeling grateful for the life that is yours. We show you how it is possible to lean toward and stay with raw, uncomfortable feelings of grief, even when you feel overwhelmed and want to run away.

Writing can help you make sense of what has happened and find meaning. We show you how to get started, even if you think you're not a writer, or you don't feel confident that you can find the right words to say what you mean.

We'll also draw upon the healing powers of making art, for both amateurs and experienced practitioners. We encourage you to embrace "beginner's mind," let go of judgments and self-criticism, and plunge in.

When painful things happen, everyone needs each other more than in ordinary times. We reflect on how grief's most unwelcome and disturbing aspects and experiences may become fertile ground for growth and change. We look at how suffering creates an opening that allows us—if and when we are ready— to connect more deeply with others and seek out and create beloved communities.

We invite you to read sequentially, or simply choose chapters that appeal to you or seem particularly appropriate to your life. Each chapter concludes with a simple meditation. We also include a few suggestions as starting points for your own explorations. These aren't intended as homework or instructions, but as simple actions or reflections to consider, leave aside, or adapt to your own experiences and interests.

In Part Two we answer questions that people often ask in Claire's bereavement groups. Their pressing concerns, along with the wish to help all who grieve, inspired the writing in this book.

In Part Three, "Deepening Practices," we offer more detail about the practices we've introduced earlier. And finally, in Part Four we include a list of favorite poems, books, and online resources.

In writing *Opening to Grief*, we are acutely aware that everyone's grief is profoundly different, and that some reflections and practices that we have chosen to write about may not speak to you at all. Or they may not speak to you now, or any time soon. Some may feel out of reach, or just not for you. We trust that you will take what's useful and let go of the rest.

We encourage you to be patient and offer yourself great kindness and compassion as you learn to trust your own compass and find your own true north.

The Well of Grief

Those who will not slip beneath
the still surface on the well of grief,
turning down through its black water
to the place we cannot breathe,
will never know the source from which we drink,
the secret water, cold and clear,
nor find in the darkness glimmering,

> *the small round coins,*

thrown by those who wished for something else.

—David Whyte

Meeting Grief
as a Companion

*All those years, I fell for the great palace lie that grief should be gotten over
as quickly and as privately as possible. But what I have discovered since is
that the lifelong fear of grief keeps us in a barren, isolated place and that only
grieving can help heal grief; the passage of time will lessen the acuteness, but
time alone, without the direct experience of grief, will not heal it.* [1]

−ANNE LAMOTT

M any of us harbor our own "great palace lies" about grief.
We may believe that grief *should* only last for a fixed
and fairly brief period of time, or that the "grieving process"
should proceed in a particular sequence.[2] In 1969, psychia-
trist and renowned researcher Elisabeth Kübler-Ross wrote a
popular book about the five stages of moving through dying
and death.[3] Decades later, Kübler-Ross and coauthor David
Kessler wrote a book in which they worked with the same
stages—denial, anger, bargaining, depression, and acceptance—to explain how people move through the grieving
experience.

Even at the time of writing *On Grief and Grieving*, the authors acknowledged that Kübler-Ross's ideas about stages were widely misunderstood.[4] She did not mean to assert that there is *only one* prescribed timeline or a *unique* sequence of emotions and experiences (denial, anger, and so forth) that most people would predictably follow as they grieved.[5]

And yet, Kübler-Ross's ideas gained traction and have continued to penetrate popular culture with far-reaching and, for some people, painful consequences. In my bereavement groups, I often hear people worry aloud that they have missed an important stage or even plaintively ask if they are grieving "correctly."

As you reflect on your own experiences, try to keep in mind that grieving has *no* predictable stages or particular timeline. Grief has as many different expressions as there are people who grieve. We all share some common and universal experiences, yet each of us moves through grief in our own way and in our own time.

GRIEF FOR LOSING ALL THAT'S DEAR

Russell Friedman, author and cofounder of the Grief Recovery Method, describes grief as "(a) *normal* and *natural* emotional reaction to loss or change of any kind."[6] Because we are human beings, we are bound to suffer heartbreaking losses. We all lose our youth. Some of us lose a child or children. We lose our parents or a partner. We lose jobs that we care about. Eventually, most of us grow old, and even the most illustrious careers come to an end. Our healthy bodies, our stuff, homes, and dreams are all temporary. Because we live fully and love, there comes a time of grieving for nearly all of us.

Grief gives rise to a rich and confusing mix of emotions and sensations anchored in sadness. This much is familiar to most of us. But fear, regret, anxiety, depression, hopelessness, despair, and anger are aspects or qualities of grief, too. And, somewhat surprisingly perhaps, so are more welcome feelings and experiences, such as gratitude and joy.

Many people feel deeply sad after the death of a loved one following a long illness. But, at the same time, it is common to hear people speak of relief—that the person who has died no longer suffers, and that their own days no longer revolve around caregiving and making complicated medical decisions.

Your grief will last for as long as it lasts. In one of my bereavement groups, two members joined the group on the same night. One had lost his partner just before joining the group, and the other had lost his spouse two years earlier. The man who had just lost his partner felt he was over the acuteness of his grief after a month and soon stopped attending. The other stayed in the group for two more years.

For some people, the hardest time is the first year following a death or major loss. You feel overwhelmed by practical tasks, such as finding a funeral home, notifying friends and family, getting through a memorial service, settling an estate, and dealing with finances and possessions. For others, the second year feels the most difficult to get through, when practical tasks that required attention (and in some ways provided respite from raw feelings) are mostly finished.

Some experience grief as a series of waves. One day you feel distraught and immobilized. The next day you find the unexpected strength to do an errand. Perhaps you walk down the aisle of a supermarket, thinking that you are having a good day. And then, you see something that reminds you of what and whom you've lost. Your heart is broken open by something as ordinary as a can of tuna.

You could think of grief as a passage. You are torn from the life you knew before. You are not who you were, and you are not yet who you will become. You are, in a very real way, between identities. This experience—profoundly different for each of us—is confusing and agonizing, and it may also be a doorway for transformation.

AN INVITATION TO GROW

Though this may be hard to believe or accept at first, grief can be seen as an invitation to grow and, eventually, to find meaning in suffering and in the experience of loss. A heart that is broken open offers a precious gift—a chance to become more authentic with yourself and with other people.

Holding grief close, as a companion, allows for opening to love, compassion, hope, and forgiveness. Author and grief therapist Francis Weller writes, "When we don't push the pain of grief away, when we welcome and engage it, we live and love more fully."[7]

MEDITATION

Sit quietly for a few moments and settle into the meditation by noticing the subtle movement in your body as you breathe in and then out. Say slowly, to yourself, the following phrases:

May I welcome all my feelings as I grieve.

May I allow grief to soften and strengthen my heart.

May I hold my sorrow with tenderness and compassion.

A Few Suggestions

Spend a few moments reflecting on any "rules" or expectations you carry about grief:

- ✒ What do you think grief *should* look like?

- ✒ How long do you think grief *should* last?

- ✒ What do you view as a normal or abnormal way to grieve?

Consider where you acquired your beliefs about grief:

- ✒ Which beliefs serve you?

- ✒ Which beliefs could you release or let go?

FROM Kindness

Before you know kindness as the deepest thing inside,
you must know sorrow as the other deepest thing.
You must wake up with sorrow.
You must speak to it till your voice
catches the thread of all sorrows
and you see the size of the cloth.

Then it is only kindness that makes sense anymore,
only kindness that ties your shoes
and sends you out into the day to mail letters
          and purchase bread,
only kindness that raises its head
from the crowd of the world to say
It is I you have been looking for,
and then goes with you everywhere
like a shadow or a friend.

—Naomi Shihab Nye

Beginning with Kindness

Be kind whenever possible. It is always possible.

−HIS HOLINESS THE DALAI LAMA

In the weeks, months, and years after a profound loss it's especially important to offer yourself great kindness. It's the best gift you can give yourself. And as it turns out, it's the best gift you can give those you love and those who love you.

How is this possible? What does it mean to be kind to yourself, to take your own side, to befriend yourself? Think about how you would reach out and be with a friend who has just suffered a loss. You would probably show up and just be there with your friend and listen to her story of all that happened. You might bring over dinners, offer to shop, ask how you might help, show her all the compassion you can muster.

Now consider what it might mean to offer these qualities of kindness to yourself who is the one hurting; also shocked; also feeling alone, hopeless, and unmoored.

How do you begin? Start wherever you are—not in some idealized place—but exactly where you're standing. Is your house a mess? Have you stopped going to the gym? Are you eating cold pizza for supper? Are you ignoring invitations from friends? Drinking or numbing yourself with other addictions? Mired in feelings of guilt or anger? With kindness, allow yourself to start here.

Perhaps you are someone who has restless energy, who likes to stay busy, who feels indispensable running from one obligation to the next, who habitually buttons up your emotions. Consider easing your schedule and giving yourself a precious gift of time: ten minutes to sit and listen to a beautiful piece of music; an evening to be alone with your discomfort and grief; or an hour for a massage.

Maybe you harbor a harsh inner critic, or perhaps a committee of judges who shame you for crying too much, grieving too long, not grieving enough, or not doing it right. Almost certainly, these voices have completely unrealistic expectations for you. Pause to notice and listen to these voices. Can you ask them to back off and give you the space to *feel* your emotions and be *with* your grief? Can you stop calling yourself a failure, a fraud, a rock, or a wimp, and offer yourself empathy and compassion? Try and drop the names and just be with the felt experience of grief in your body.

Can you embrace your vulnerability, your irritability, your impatience, and even your resistance as deeply human responses to separation and loss? Can you see how being open and tender with yourself allows you to better understand and connect with others—those who hurt and those who haven't yet experienced pain and hardship?

If you look deeply and sit with pain and suffering, can you feel how "normal" sorrow is, how it is a precious part of being human?

Can you see how kindness—which includes being kind to yourself, seeing yourself as part of a larger community of people who all bear their own sorrow—*is* a path through grief to a life you might not yet be able to imagine? Can you acknowledge yourself and say thank you for ways you *are* taking care of yourself, for surviving, for the small steps you have taken, for moments of joy or moments of finding some comfort amid tears?

A Practice of Loving-Kindness

Metta, or loving-kindness practice, comes from Buddhist and Hindu traditions. It's a rich practice that offers a way of befriending ourselves and all living beings. We introduce the basics here and explore *metta* in more detail in Part Three called "Deepening Practices."

To begin, sit and silently repeat this series of blessings, starting with yourself:

May I welcome all my feelings as I grieve.
May I allow grief to soften and strengthen my heart.
May I hold my sorrow with tenderness and compassion.

Next, offer these same blessings to someone who gladdens your heart, someone to whom you can easily extend good wishes. Then, widen the circle and extend these wishes to some-one about whom you feel neutral (neither friendly nor hostile), and finally, extend these wishes to a person you find difficult or challenging. As you bring each person to mind, sit quietly and silently offer these blessings.

May you be deeply peaceful.
May you be happy and healthy.
May you live with ease.

Conclude by offering *metta* to all living beings. You might want to begin locally, for example, by extending blessings to everyone in your home or apartment building, then to everyone in your neighborhood or in your town. Then, imagine extending blessings to everyone in your state, country, and finally, across the globe, with these words:

May all beings be deeply peaceful.
May all beings be happy and healthy.
May all beings live with ease.

You may want to choose a series of *metta* blessings that speak directly to your experience of grief. For example:

May I be open to all the difficult and painful emotions and sensations of grief.

May I forgive myself for mistakes I've made or for words not said.

May I offer myself compassion.

If these blessings don't resonate with you, choose your own phrases and modify them as you practice.

MEDITATION

Sit quietly for a few moments and unify your attention, noticing the subtle movement of your body as you breathe. Gently follow the natural flow of your breath, in and out. If possible for you, choose a chair or cushion that supports you sitting upright, with relaxed but erect posture. If you are more comfortable, sit on a couch or bed. Silently and slowly say the following phrases to yourself:

May I start right here.
May I offer myself kindness and compassion.
May I accept myself as I am.

A Few Suggestions

Take a few minutes and reflect on ways of offering yourself kindness today:

If you're always busy, take a few minutes and do something relaxing, such as reading a poem or listening to a piece of music you love.

If you harbor an inner critic who shames you for not grieving the right way, try responding to one of the critic's accusations by saying, "I'm doing the best I can," or "Over time, things will get easier." Or choose another mantra or phrase that helps you feel supported.

In my own worst seasons I've come back from the colorless world of despair by forcing myself to look hard, for a long time, at a single glorious thing: a flame of red geranium outside my bedroom window. And then another: my daughter in a yellow dress. And another: the perfect outline of a full, dark sphere behind the crescent moon. Until I learned to be in love with my life again. Like a stroke victim retraining new parts of the brain to grasp lost skills, I have taught myself joy, over and over again.

—Barbara Kingsolver

Feeling Grateful

A Personal Reflection

I keep a journal beside my bed. Some nights, instead of writing,
I whisper my gratitude. I know that someone, somewhere is listening.

I'm grateful that the loss of my breast (from cancer)
has unearthed my beating heart and made it visible to me.

I'm grateful for the roof over my head.

I'm grateful I have enough money for tomorrow.

−JACKIE

A growing body of research links feeling grateful with being happier.[1] When we stop to appreciate our blessings, we tap into positive emotions. We counter an ancient bias toward the negative that was once useful for the survival of our species, and instead we cultivate a greater sense of well-being.

CREATING A POSITIVE CYCLE

Neuropsychologist, meditation teacher, and author Rick Hanson explains that our brain has a negativity bias that has evolved from our earliest ancestors, who constantly had to scan for threatening situations in order to stay alive. In our modern lives, we're no longer called on to fight tigers, and yet this predisposition to take in and remember negative experiences persists.

Negative experiences, Hanson says, adhere to our brains like glue and color our internal landscape toward focusing on what's wrong. We remember bad dentist visits when we were kids, or the time we fell off our bike and had to be taken to the emergency room, or when our first boyfriend or girlfriend dumped us for someone else. Though we might forget some of the details, we tend to remember and hold onto the feelings we had.

As you might guess, more enjoyable and positive experiences are much less likely to stick. They flow over us like water, hardly registering in our memories. Given the brain's negativity bias, "it takes an *active* effort to internalize positive experiences and heal negative ones," Hanson writes. "When you tilt toward what's positive, you're actually righting a neurological imbalance."[2]

Hanson invites us to begin by noticing good things, even small experiences that happen to us throughout the day. Perhaps you watched a lovely sunrise or sunset. Or, someone unexpectedly came over to visit, you solved a difficult problem, someone hugged you, or you felt a sense of belonging.

Hanson suggests that we take time to pause before jumping to the next thing, pay attention to these satisfying experiences, dwell on them for twenty or thirty seconds, and bring them inside so they may stay with us. "Imagine or feel that the experience is entering deeply into your mind and body, like the sun's warmth into a T-shirt, water into a sponge, or a jewel placed in a treasure chest in your heart. Keep relaxing your body and absorbing the emotions, sensations, and thoughts of the experience."[3]

By making a deliberate effort to bring in the good, we can actually rewire our brains. By building on the good feelings we generate today, we increase the likelihood of positive feelings and well-being tomorrow.

KEEPING A GRATITUDE JOURNAL

Writing in a gratitude journal—in which you note things large and small that you appreciate and that make your day better—is one way of cultivating gratitude and helping yourself generate a spirit of contentment for what *is*, rather than longing for what you don't have.

Begin by thinking of a few pleasant experiences that occurred, or gifts that you received, throughout your day. As you recall these moments, linger with them and notice particular details, recalling different sensations (such as smells or touch), thoughts, and feelings. Take a moment to imagine what your life would be like without these kindnesses or this beauty.

See if you can be grateful for all the ways you are supported by other people and by the Earth's bounty. Can you expand your awareness to feeling grateful for clean water, healthy food, a comfortable home, your education, family members, and friends?

MEDITATION

Sit quietly for a few moments, noticing the subtle flow of your breathing, in and out. When you feel settled, say slowly, to yourself, the following phrases:

> May I pause and notice what's good in my life.
> May I open all my senses to my blessings.
> May I remember to offer thanks.

A Few Suggestions

Write to someone and let them know you are grateful for something they have done:

- Write an email or a note to someone who came by to tell them you appreciated their visit.

- Write a letter (whether or not you send it—this exercise is for *you*) thanking someone whose presence has made a profound difference in your life.

Begin a gratitude journal:

- Recall two or three things that happened today for which you feel grateful.

- You might note something simple like the car starting right away so you could easily be on time for your appointment.

- Or you might write about big things that you're thankful for, like having a healthy body or feeling a deep sense of belonging.

Linger with a meal:

- Consider the sources of your food, the many hands that made it possible, the elements of nature that allowed it to grow, and the ways this meal nourishes you.

ENOUGH . . . .

Enough. These few words are enough.
If not these words, this breath.
If not this breath, this sitting here.
This opening to the life
we have refused
again and again
until now.
Until now.

—David Whyte

Opening to Mindfulness and Meditation

A Personal Reflection

My son Daniel was thirty when he died in a climbing accident. Although I'd been living alone for many years, I found it unbearable after Dan's death to come home to an empty house. Every evening after work, I would drop in on friends, or go to a movie, or eat alone in a crowded restaurant. Most nights I'd find a bar where I could sit until closing time. Before long it took an extra drink to numb the feeling of desolation that was waiting to greet me when I unlocked the front door.

All this busyness was a distraction, but I couldn't seem to stop. I had a vague sense of yearning for something more satisfying, but I didn't know what it was. When a coworker suggested I attend her meditation class, I reluctantly agreed to try.

At first, I couldn't sit still, even for ten minutes. My mind raced. I spoke to the instructor, who suggested that I try connecting some words to my breath to help focus my mind. I can't say exactly how long it took— maybe a month—before I noticed that my restlessness was easing and I felt a sense of settling inside myself.

I started to meditate at home for five minutes each morning.
Then after a few weeks, I sat a little longer. I began to see that time as
wrapping my arms around my heart.

—JOHN

When you try to turn away from grief, when you hope to bypass or escape it, grief persists. Painful emotions—such as sadness, anger, or fear—linger and may even seem worse than ever. Until you stop running, begin to name or acknowledge and lean into all you've been through, and build a friendly relationship with grief, you'll almost certainly continue to suffer.

Alan Wolfelt, author, educator, and grief counselor, puts it this way: " . . . the pain that surrounds the *closed* heart of grief is the pain of living against yourself, the pain of denying how the loss changes you, the pain of feeling alone and isolated—unable to openly mourn, unable to love and be loved by those around you."[1]

What would it mean to live instead with an *open* heart, denying none of your pain or grief, mourning in whatever ways feel appropriate and comforting, being loving and loved by those around you?

Perhaps you're already familiar with meditation and mindfulness. These rich practices can open a doorway into compassionate awareness and understanding that might resonate with you and support you.

STARTING WITH THE BREATH

We invite you to try a basic sitting meditation of being mindful of your breath and the subtle movements in your body as you're breathing. The idea is simple: Sit quietly and rest your attention on your breath, which is always there, always changing, moment by moment. As you inhale and exhale, see if you are able to feel the unique sensations of each breath. Breathing in, breathing out, breathing in, breathing out.

Find a quiet place to sit, either on a chair with your feet on the floor, or, if you prefer, on a meditation cushion, or on your couch or bed. You may wish to close your eyes or soften your gaze and look at the floor in front of you. If possible, sit in a relaxed and upright posture with a comfortably straight spine, and place your hands on your thighs.

You might think meditating while being aware of your breathing will be easy. Most people, however, find they're barely able to sustain their attention for one or two inhalation-exhalation cycles before they get distracted. We're always thinking. Our minds dart to a to-do list, to what occurred earlier at work, to whether we like meditation, or to any of a thousand places, emotions, and sensations. When this happens, as it will again and again, try to maintain a non-judging and curious attitude and gently bring your attention back to your breath, back to the present moment. Offer yourself patience and encouragement, no matter how you think you're doing.

Notice whatever you notice. You may want to bring your attention to feeling your breath at your nostrils: the cool air coming in, and the warmer air on your upper lip as you are breathing out. Or you may feel your chest and belly expanding and softening on the in-breath and gently drawing back toward your spine on the outbreath. Some people like to feel their whole body breathing. As your body becomes quiet and relaxed, you might even feel and hear your heart beating.

If you are someone who has difficulty sitting still, or if you can't tame your wild, scattered mind, hope is not lost! There are other ways to meditate, such as walking meditation, that might suit you better. In walking meditation, you bring your attention to your feet as you take each step.

To begin, maintain a relaxed, soft gaze toward the floor in front of you and walk *very* slowly across a short distance (of perhaps thirty or forty feet), noticing all the sensations in your feet and legs, step after step. Take one full breath with each step, and bring your awareness to each part of your foot that touches the floor—your heel, the ball of your foot, then your toes. Notice sensations as you lift your foot to take your next step and again feel your heel and other parts of your foot touching the floor.

Slowly turn around when you reach the far end of the space you have chosen for yourself; then return, step by step, to your starting point. Continue, paying relaxed and concentrated attention, until the end of your meditation session.

Don't be surprised or discouraged if it takes weeks or months (or even years) before you *begin* to get the hang of meditation, no matter which approach you choose. Meditation is called a practice, because it takes understanding, repetition, and a kind of relaxed discipline to cultivate what is a new and profound habit. Many find it helpful to read an introductory meditation or mindfulness book, or to start with a class led by an experienced teacher, and then practice with a meditation group or community.

STEADYING THE MIND

Perhaps now is a good time to address the *why* of practicing meditation. Why pursue something that feels so unfamiliar, that's challenging, and perhaps feels pointless or boring? How might a meditation practice be useful in a time of intense suffering?

The best short and beginning answer is that meditating helps you steady your mind. When you concentrate on a single domain or object, such as your breath or the sensations in your feet, you are gathering your attention and training your mind to become calmer and more stable. As your mind becomes steadier, you're able to attend not only to an object like your breath, but also to be aware of other sensations (sight, sounds, touch), as well as to your thoughts and emotions, to your mind and your body—to all your experiences.

Mindfulness—paying attention in a particular way to *all* that's happening in the present moment—allows you to pause, and to clarify and focus your thoughts (develop insight), and to feel your feelings. Then, (with practice) you have an opportunity to respond wisely and compassionately to whatever is happening (good or bad) with skill, freedom, and peace of mind.

MINDFULNESS IN EVERY MOMENT

Most of us, if we notice it and admit it, spend our time living on autopilot. We ruminate on the past, worry about what might (or might not) happen in the future, and pay little attention to what we're experiencing in the present moment. We spin along and react to each thing we encounter, missing out on the depth, texture, and meaning of our lives.

Mindfulness is a way of living and being that might be new to you. It's simple, and yet at the same time it's profound and not easy. Renowned mindfulness practitioner and author Jon Kabat-Zinn describes mindfulness as a purposeful and compassionate way of paying attention, moment by moment.

Mindfulness has the quality of being nonjudgmental. When you are being mindful, you try to let go of judgments about whether you like or don't like what's happening, whether something is good or bad, easy or difficult. Instead of struggling with your preferences and desires, your hatreds and frustrations, you try to meet experience *as it is*.[2]

Mindfulness also has the quality of being openhearted. As you practice mindfulness, you maintain a kind, loving presence toward yourself, no matter how you're doing or how you feel. The intention of mindfulness is to create a safe, welcoming space that extends to our imperfect selves the same qualities of compassion and acceptance we would offer a dear friend.

Many begin practicing mindfulness while sitting in meditation. As you become more experienced, you are able to bring mindfulness to more aspects of your life. You don't need to do anything special. You can practice everywhere: on the couch, driving the car, doing the dishes, walking, cooking or eating a meal, or sitting at your desk—all with the intention of bringing your mind and body together in the same place at the same time.

You draw your attention to sensations in your body, as well as to your thoughts and emotions as they arise. Gradually, you notice ways that you seek and grasp onto pleasant experiences and try to suppress or avoid unpleasant experiences. You see how you struggle, respond unskillfully, and create unnecessary suffering for yourself and others. And you begin to catch a glimmer of a more mindful, more awake, freer way to live!

When we bring an attitude of mindfulness to grief and suffering, we try to look clearly at, and experience directly, everything that has happened, just *as it is*. We allow or make room for it all—including experiences and feelings we don't want.

Let's say, for example, that you're overwhelmed by anger. Try to just sit with anger's uncomfortable feelings and sensations. See if you can get in touch with ways that anger (even though it may feel empowering in the short run) might mask another emotion or vulnerability that sits underneath anger and is even more challenging (such as hurt, betrayal, or abandonment). To the best of your ability, try to hold yourself tenderly and make space for everything that arises, one day at a time.

(We note here that some people experience anxiety—even terror—as they sit in meditation and stillness, perhaps for the first time. If this is true for you, try not to push yourself beyond your comfort level or limit. Instead, experiment with dipping in and out of difficult territory in order to titrate your experience. Consider whether to consult with a mental health professional or seek guidance from an experienced meditation teacher.)

Being mindful is a way of listening deeply to our inner voice, and of connecting with strengths and vulnerabilities. Instead of turning away, we include or allow all our feelings—regret, fear, confusion, anxiety, sorrow, as well as joy, exuberance, happiness, and hope. We return home fully to ourselves, just as we are.[3] Mindfulness helps us remember to pause, take time out from the daily demands of our lives, calm our minds—and to sit with and bear raw grief.

"Personal times of stillness are a spiritual necessity," writes Alan Wolfelt. "Stillness restores your life force. Grief is only transformed when you honor the quiet forces of stillness."[4] In stillness, we begin to reassemble our shattered lives. We find the strength to face suffering, to open to the changes that grief has brought, to remember and celebrate those we've lost, and to honor what is most deeply true in our loved ones and ourselves.

MEDITATION

Sit quietly for a few moments, noticing the subtle movement of your body as you breathe. Say slowly, to yourself, the following phrases:

May I allow moments of quiet and stillness.
May I feel my breath as I breathe in.
May I feel my breath as I breathe out.
As I open to grief, may I hold my suffering tenderly.

A Few Suggestions

Find a quiet place and practice a short walking meditation:

- Choose a place indoors or outdoors where you can walk mindfully for five or ten minutes.

- Take one full breath, in and out, with each step, bringing your awareness to each part of your foot as it touches the ground.

Find a quiet place and practice a short listening meditation:

- Set a timer for five minutes.

- Sit in a comfortable, relaxed position.

- Simply listen to sounds around you.

- Notice and be with whatever you hear, without judging whether you like it or not.

- Notice the sensations in your body.

Eat a meal in mindfulness:

- Sit down where it's quiet, where there are no distractions from digital devices.

- ✐ Draw your attention to your food: its colors, textures, and smells.

- ✐ Chew and swallow each bite slowly, and allow yourself to linger with its taste.

The Peace of Wild Things

*When despair for the world grows in me
and I wake in the night at the least sound
in fear of what my life and my children's lives may be,
I go and lie down where the wood drake
rests in his beauty on the water, and the great heron feeds.
I come into the peace of wild things
who do not tax their lives with forethought
of grief. I come into the presence of still water.
And I feel above me the day-blind stars
waiting with their light. For a time
I rest in the grace of the world, and am free.*

—*Wendell Berry*

Restoring in Nature

Sorrow is part of the Earth's great cycles, flowing into the night like cool air sinking down a river course. To feel sorrow is to float on the pulse of the Earth, the surge from living to dying, from coming into being to ceasing to exist. Maybe this is why the Earth has the power over time to wash sorrow into a deeper pool, cold and shadowed. And maybe this is why, even though sorrow never disappears, it can make a deeper connection to the currents of life and so connect, somehow, to sources of wonder and solace.[1]

—KATHLEEN DEAN MOORE

We live in a paradox. Humans have an instinct to bond and affiliate with other life-forms. This is what renowned evolutionary biologist E. O. Wilson writes about in *Biophilia*: "From infancy we concentrate happily on ourselves and other organisms. We learn to distinguish life from the inanimate and move toward it like moths to a porch light . . . our existence depends on this propensity, our spirit is woven from it, hope rises on its currents."[2]

And yet, elements of our fast-moving culture undeniably weaken our connection with the natural world. The immediacy and intensity of technology distract us, as Richard Louv writes in *The Nature Principle: Reconnecting with Life in a Virtual Age*. We witness parents struggling to limit their young children's screen time and to persuade their kids to go outdoors. We see kids who don't know what to do when they're asked to put their hands in soil and plant a garden.

As adults, we tie ourselves to computers and mostly work indoors. Even when we're outside, we're tethered to cell phones and handheld devices. Navigating traffic; making split-second decisions; meeting deadlines; responding to emails, tweets, and texts—all these activities bombard us and highjack our attention.

When we experience loss, when we are grieving, it is more important than ever to find ways back to the garden, to spend time in the healing power of nature. Psychologists Rachel and Steven Kaplan research and write about the benefits of "restorative environments"[3]: outdoor places that are accessible, quiet, and relatively small, such as your yard, or a pocket park in a city. And if there is no safe outdoor space where you live, if you are confined indoors, even in a hospital bed, you can rest in nature just looking out a window to a patch of sky, or gazing at a plant indoors.

When we spend time in restorative places, it becomes effortless to watch leaves floating down from trees, to notice a reflection of the sky in a puddle, or to hear a bird call. These environments draw us in without asking us to focus on anything special. There's nothing to do. When we return to focused cognitive tasks (like writing a report or solving a problem), we feel refreshed.

We all enjoy nature for our own reasons. Some of us love solitude. Instead of feeling lonely, we find ourselves in nature. Some of us feel connected when we are in an environment larger than ourselves. Some adventure into wild realms; others sit on benches by meadows not far from home, or rest on the seat of their walker. Some feel within us the seasonal cycles of life and death.

Across Canada, people have formed walking groups to help with grief. They gather, stand together, and share memories. Some cry. No one tries to fix anything. They just meet and listen to each other. And then they walk together, one step at a time.[4]

Could you commit to sitting outdoors ten minutes a day, as the weather permits? Paying attention with all your senses—sight, sound, touch, taste, smell—what do you begin to notice? Can you feel the breeze blowing across your face right now, just now? Watch a cloud moving, just now? Feel your breath, in and out, each breath different and fresh, just now?

If you can't get outside into nature today, can you remember experiences in childhood when you lost yourself outdoors—when you first learned to row a boat or build a shelter in the woods, or when you first saw fireflies on a humid summer evening? Do you have a photograph of yourself as a toddler sitting on a beach, running through a sprinkler, or learning to ride a bike?

Does your day include walks with your dog? Are you passionate about biking, birding, hiking, or fishing? Do you like to visit a gravesite or drive to a beautiful spot for a picnic? Are you a gardener? If you don't have your own plot, would you consider signing up for a space in a community garden? Could a friend take you for a drive along quiet streets? Could you just look out the car window?

MEDITATION

Sit quietly for a few moments, resting in the feeling and flow of your breathing, in and out. Say slowly, to yourself, the following phrases:

May I allow nature to restore my spirit.

May I find comfort in the presence of animals.

May I notice rhythms of death and renewal all around me.

A Few Suggestions

Spend some time in nature:

- Using *all your senses*, notice what's around you.
- Listen to whatever sounds arise and fade, feel the breeze on your skin, or smell fresh grass or decaying leaves.
- Dwell on these sensations for a few minutes.

Look for something in the natural world that seems to reflect your grief:

- 🖉 Consider nature's cycle: life, death, decay, rebirth, restoration, and rejuvenation.

- 🖉 Can you sense nature's transforming power?

Spend some time with animals:

- 🖉 Go for a walk with a dog or volunteer at an animal shelter.

- 🖉 Watch and play with your cat.

- 🖉 Sit outside and watch birds flying or squirrels burying acorns.

SHELTER

She built a hut
Out of rushes and mud
At the side of the road
And sat down to mourn
Her life alone,
Villagers came by
In ones and twos to touch
Her hand, bring plates
Of food, and tell
Their stories. So did
The mourner's hut become
A shelter for the town.

—Robin S. Chapman

Joining Together

The friend who can be silent with us in a moment of despair or confusion,
who can stay with us in an hour of grief and bereavement, who can
tolerate not knowing . . . not healing . . . not curing . . .
that is a friend who cares.[1]

—HENRI NOUWEN

We all need other people, never more than when we're overwhelmed by grief. We need one another to stay sane, to feel that we belong, to take a break, to fix a leaking toilet, to watch a movie together, to talk about the unspeakable events that just happened, to sing, to cry, and to laugh out loud. We need a check-in with a friend, a walk, tea, a kindness, the presence of another human being who listens and reminds us that everything changes, and that someday we'll feel more ease.

We may not like being the person who needs a lifeline, the person who admits her sorrow is more than she can bear alone. But at times, it's our turn to be the one receiving casseroles, flowers, and phone calls just to see if we're okay. That's how it is. And another day, it will be someone else's turn, and we'll be the one driving up to their house, bringing dinner, looking after their kids, just showing up. Isn't it true that the more generosity you can take in, the more you have to give?

Big losses—even when they're expected, as when someone dies after a prolonged illness—shock most of us to the core. Losses counted in the hundreds of thousands of lives, as in the pandemic, cause us to question our safety and our very existence. No wonder we become numb, distraught, lost, barely able to function—not ourselves.

When you are overcome with grief, it is common to take time apart for a while, maybe even for a long while, to go inside to be with your grief, to rest, and to heal.

But then what? How and when is it possible to re-engage? What if you finally feel ready to connect—at least for that moment—and an hour later decide it isn't what you want after all? What you really want is to stay home, because you don't have the energy to be with friends, or you don't want to break open or cry in public. Maybe you dread feeling invisible if no one mentions your loss, or you simply feel afraid to leave the house. Like many people, we swing back and forth, not sure when it's better to push through fears or when it's okay to yield and keep to ourselves.

Sometimes, we take a tentative step to reach out, and then discover that friends who were attentive during the first few weeks after our loss have returned to their own lives. Perhaps they assume we're doing better and don't need their help, or they feel uncomfortable around sadness or despair. For whatever reasons, they're less available.

What can be a lifeline at such a time? Some people seek out a "grief friend," a person at church or work, or a neighbor who understands that grief doesn't go away, and who is willing to sit and listen as we cry, rage, laugh, and tell and retell our story.

Some people seek out a bereavement group where they sit with people who are also suffering and know the experiences they're going through. Some people find a group that includes people with a variety of experiences of loss. Others choose a bereavement group with a focus, for example: a group for young adults who have lost a parent; or one for people affected by suicide; or one for caregivers of someone with dementia or cancer; or one for people mourning their pets.

Maybe you have joined a support group and heard someone say he talks with his departed partner, and you say to yourself, "I do that, too!" You listen to a person tell the group that he goes into his closet to smell his partner's clothes. Or you hear someone say she can't bear to give her partner's clothes away because she believes (as author Joan Didion did) that her spouse may come back from the dead and need his shoes.[2] And you laugh and think, "Me, too!"

Perhaps week after week, you sit with the same people in your bereavement group, and one day you realize you are part of a beloved community.

The Alchemy of Transforming Suffering

We've all heard of courageous people who, after experiencing a painful loss, transform their suffering into passion, purpose, and community. The word *passion* derives from the Latin *passus*, meaning to suffer. Guided by a desire to help others avoid the suffering they've experienced, they devote themselves to a cause larger than themselves.

Candy Lightner, whose daughter was killed by a drunk driver, started the group Mothers Against Drunk Driving (MADD). Haven Fyfe-Kiernan, who lost her husband on the first plane that crashed into the North Tower of the World Trade Center, opened The Wellness Room in Massachusetts to offer bereavement counseling. The parents of Matthew Shepard, who was brutally murdered for being gay, became strong advocates for lesbian, gay, bisexual, transgender, questioning, and/or queer (LGBTQ) rights and helped pass a federal law called the Hate Crimes Prevention Act (HCPA).

And there is the extraordinary example of His Holiness the Dalai Lama, who fled his homeland at the outset of the 1959 Tibetan uprising against Chinese occupation. His Holiness embodies the losses and suffering of the Tibetan people, while also exuding kindness, love, and joy wherever he goes.

Granted, these are remarkable responses to unspeakable losses, but there are lots of examples of ordinary people who also act with great joy, kindness, and generosity, at least in part because they too have suffered and want to give something back. When one of my bereavement groups was ending, a widower named Charles joined a new bereavement group. He was beginning to feel happier and more rooted, and he believed his experiences could be a beacon of hope to those newly bereaved.

Some people join choruses that sing at the bedsides of the dying.[3] Others volunteer at local shelters to walk dogs and reduce the suffering of animals waiting for adoption, or ride their bikes to raise money for charitable causes. Volunteers with the National Alliance on Mental Illness (NAMI) work to create housing for adults affected with mental illness. A mother who lost her baby at birth raises money for her hospital's neonatal unit—hoping to save another family from the tragedy she suffered.

How will you take your broken-open heart, your vulnerability and your tenderness, and allow it to restore your own well-being? At some point when you're ready, and only when you are ready and have enough energy to reach out, how will you allow your grieving heart to connect with others and make the world a little more welcoming?

MEDITATION

Sit quietly for a few moments, noticing the feeling and flow of your breathing, in and out. Say slowly, to yourself, the following phrases:

> May I allow myself to feel vulnerable.
> May I have the courage to ask for what I need.
> May I find ways to help other people and other living beings.

A Few Suggestions

Reflect on ways you might develop a support network for yourself:

- Reach out to someone today to see if they would be a "grief friend."
- Look for a local bereavement group or an online community that can support you.

Take a few minutes to reflect on activities you love, such as making music, woodworking, learning a language, or playing sports:

- What small gesture can you make to cultivate one or more of these passions, foster community, and give back?

- Identify someone who is struggling because of a difficult relationship, a sick child, stress at work, or homelessness.

- What random act of kindness might you offer?

Let yourself be silently drawn
by the strange pull of what you really love.
It will not lead you astray.
—Rumi

Making Art

Loss makes artists of us all as we weave new patterns
in the fabric of our lives.

−GRETA CROSBY

Do you remember when your third-grade teacher asked you to write a poem or a story or draw a picture? Do you remember that most of us just did it without much thought? As kids, we knew how to draw pictures and feel delight in what we had done. With complete abandon, we could sing a song or dance in front of others. Most of us could move our bodies freely without feeling an ounce of self-consciousness.

Rarely a day goes by when my five-year-old granddaughter, Ruby, doesn't make something. She has a small table in the living room where she keeps crayons, markers, paper, scissors, and glue. Ruby doesn't scrutinize her own work. She declares what she will draw and draws it. Then, without apology, she shows her mother or father what she's done.

When did we stop making stuff for the pure joy of it? When did we stop thinking of ourselves as creative? When did we start telling ourselves that we don't have enough experience or talent, or that no one will take us seriously?

Did we give away our creative DNA? Did we allow our artistic expression to be taken away from us? Was it educated out of us? How did we develop such a narrow and critical vision of what art and creativity are that we could so easily exclude ourselves? And how can we reclaim our artistic expression, our creative juices?

Is this a time—when your heart is broken and you're grieving—that you can find solace in art? Perhaps choose to make something that speaks directly to your grief, such as a sacred altar, a collage, or a quilt made of strips of your lover's clothing? Or choose a project that has little to do with suffering, but emerges from other memories and joys, from something you've always wanted to explore? Can you find comfort in feeling the wetness of clay as you learn to throw a pot on a wheel, in seeing beauty through the lens of a camera, in touching the keys of a piano, in creating a new recipe, tuning a guitar, or just doodling?

For many of us, it is uncomfortable or frustrating to try something new, or to return to a creative practice such as dancing or playing an instrument in which you once excelled but are no longer accomplished. "You might be scared to start. That's natural," writes Austin Kleon in *Steal Like an Artist*.[1] The ground under your feet doesn't feel solid. Not knowing what you're doing, you might feel like a fake.

When you first start making art, will you stumble? Probably. Perhaps you have an image in your mind's eye of how fantastic it will be to knit your first sweater, and then it turns out lumpy. You dream of playing a beautiful piece—Haydn's "Trumpet Concerto in E-flat major"—but your lip hurts and you have to stop after ten minutes. You're making a delicate cut for a stained-glass project, inspired by a heron on a lovely wetland, and the glass shatters. Disappointed, you question why you ever thought about trying something creative, why you invested in materials or committed to a studio or a daily practice.

Try to quell those internal voices shouting, "failure." Remind yourself that it's okay to "fail," that it is even good to fail, and that failing is part of what it means to create or succeed; that it's the process or the journey that matters, not the result. Feeling more hopeful, or determined, consider signing up for a workshop, finding a coach, a guide, or others who may support you.

See if you can take comfort in the word *amateur* as someone who creates something because they love it, because they view their art as a gift to themselves and to those they care about.

Imagine yourself after a few weeks immersed in making things. Your days feel richer. If you're lucky enough to find a community of weavers, photographers, or knitters, you might dare share your insecurities, or what you've created. Some of these new people may even become your friends.

Poet, author, and teacher Jane Hirshfield describes the relationship between suffering, grief, and art: "We make art, I believe, partly because our lives are ungraspable, uncarryable, impossible to navigate without it. Even our joys are vanishing things, subject to transience. How, then, could there be any beauty without some awareness of loss, of suffering? The surprising thing is that the opposite is also true, that suffering leads us to beauty the way thirst leads us to water . . . . Art isn't a superficial addition to our lives; it's as necessary as oxygen. Amid the cliffs and abysses every life brings, art allows us to find a way to agree to suffering, to include it and not be broken, to say *yes* to what actually is, and then to say something further, something that changes and opens the heart, the ears, the eyes, the mind."[2]

As you continue making things, it no longer matters whether you're able to write a perfect song, whether your film gets into a film festival, or whether you become an accomplished artist. What's important is doing the work, being in the arena, walking toward the mountain.[3]

MEDITATION

Sit quietly for a few moments, noticing the feeling and flow of your breath, in and out. Say slowly, to yourself, the following phrases:

May I relax my inner critic.
May I allow myself to be a beginner.
May I find joy and meaning in making art.

A Few Suggestions

Give yourself permission to be inspired:

- When it's possible, go to an exhibit or spend an hour browsing in a bookstore. Listen to a podcast or watch a film.

- Gather materials and ideas for a project you'd like to start.

Try making something today:

- Sketch or take a photo, doodle, arrange some flowers, write a haiku poem, strum your guitar, dance, or work in any medium that gives you pleasure.

What's In My Journal

Odd things, like a button drawer. Mean
things, fishhooks, barbs in your hand.
But marbles too. A genius for being agreeable.
Junkyard crucifixes, voluptuous
discards. Space for knickknacks, and for
Alaska. Evidence to hang me, or to beatify.
Clues that lead nowhere, that never connected
anyway. Deliberate obfuscation, the kind
that takes genius. Chasms in character.
Loud omissions. Mornings that yawn above
a new grave. Pages you know exist
but you can't find them. Someone's terribly
inevitable life story, maybe mine.

—William Stafford

Writing as a Refuge

Had I been blessed with even limited access to my own mind
there would have been no reason to write. I write entirely to find out
what I'm thinking, what I'm looking at, what I see and what it means.
What I want and what I fear.[1]

–JOAN DIDION

For author Joan Didion, writing is as natural and essential as breathing. So, it's no surprise that writing was her refuge in the months after her husband died suddenly from cardiac arrest. *The Year of Magical Thinking* is Didion's beautiful and heartbreaking memoir, her reporting from the raw front lines of her grief.

In a time of loss and grief, sitting down and writing may offer a sanctuary, not just for authors and experienced wordsmiths, but for the rest of us, too. There's an extensive body of research about how writing can help.[2]

EXPRESSIVE WRITING

A few decades ago, psychologist James Pennebaker pioneered what has become a robust field of study and practice called expressive, or therapeutic, writing.

Pennebaker and his colleagues showed that writing can be helpful for those who have been through traumatic and emotionally challenging experiences that are hard to share. The research showed improvements in the health and well-being of those participants in an experimental group who were asked to write (expressing their deepest thoughts and feelings about a traumatic event) for three or four consecutive days, for fifteen to thirty minutes each day.[3]

Pennebaker explains that when we write about these events, we have the chance to describe, organize, and structure disturbing experiences into a story that helps us understand the complexity of what has happened to us. "In the same story we can talk both about the cause of the event and its many implications. . . . Once a complex event is put into a story format, it is simplified. The mind doesn't need to work as hard to bring structure and meaning to it."[4]

Keeping It Simple

Many of us were told at some time in our lives that we can't write. Maybe this happened in middle school, or you were criticized by a parent, or in a college writing class. And you've come to believe it. We may harbor a critical inner voice like an old ghost that tells us we're a fraud, not good enough, and we're never going to find the words we need or put them in the right order. If this is the case for you, try throwing these harsh old voices a bone and ask them to respectfully quiet down!

If you feel stuck, start with something simple. Write a list of all the emotions you're feeling, or of what you need to do this week, or of what you can imagine unfolding in the next few months, or of people you can call on, or of ways to get out of the house. If none of these ideas resonate with you, choose something that does.

A Grief Journal

Consider writing in a grief journal—a notebook or computer file—that's private and meant just for you. Maybe start with just a few words, even a sentence describing how hard it is to get started. Write about how your morning is going, or isn't. As you feel more comfortable and discover something interesting, you might write more. Write whatever comes to mind—without stopping or editing yourself. Keep your hand or fingers moving, and write.

Writing a Note or an Email

Think about sending an appreciative note or email to someone who was kind or especially helpful to you—a relative, friend, doctor, hospice nurse, or caregiver.

You might even find solace, connection, and joy in writing a letter to a loved one who is no longer here. A man in one of my bereavement groups writes a letter to his partner every Thursday, because that was the day of the week she died.

When you write—even though you don't intend to actually send the letter—your words help you to stay connected with, and to linger with, the dear person you've lost: who they were, what you loved together, the conversations you shared, and the precious gifts you want to carry forward.

An Un-mailed Letter to a Partner Who Died

Dear Jim,

What a glorious morning! Sunny and cold (9 degrees), freshly fallen snow. I went cross-country skiing on the rail trail—beautiful and peaceful. The only company was a pair of deer that leapt across the trail in front of me. Breaking a trail on the new soft snow, feeling wonderful to be outside in the quiet where we walked together so often (and for once I was dressed in just enough layers—half of which were yours, half mine). I felt myself smiling, moving through the snow. I felt you with me. I hadn't taken skis out the last two winters, last winter not enough snow and the winter before too much and my focus on being with you. I was happy to be skiing again, appreciating the stillness.

With much love and gratitude,
—Debbie

Writing Your Personal Story

Whether you're an accomplished writer or just want to try something new, you might choose to write your own story, your deeply personal account of what you've suffered and been through and where you are today.

We're all drawn to stories. Some say that storytelling is in our genes and is basic, just like language itself. As children, we listen to and tell stories. Later, we learn to read fiction and non-fiction stories. We spend countless hours watching stories on TV and plugging in to social media. Even advertising celebrates and exploits our love affair with stories.

Consider for a moment the shape of many compelling stories. Often there's a sympathetic character facing a dilemma that upsets his peace of mind or equilibrium. He's burdened by something, or wants something he doesn't have.

This initiates a plot or a series of connected events. As a reader, you turn page after page, staying on board because you want to know what will happen next. As the story unfolds, the character makes a plan, stumbles, tries something different, and then reaches a turning point where she learns something. She grows, changes, and arrives at a different place from where she started.

Do you begin to see how this relates to your own story about grief and suffering? Might writing a personal narrative help you find meaning? You sit at your desk, or if it's possible, you go to the library or a café, and you spend time sifting through the metaphorical rubble. You pay attention to details you might have overlooked. You recall conversations. And you bear witness to what you were thinking and feeling and how you acted in different moments.

By writing your story, you discover connections, explore underlying ideas and emotions, see where and how you struggled, take measure of the obstacles you faced, what you could control and what you couldn't. As you write and reflect, you might discover negative stories you've been telling yourself about the part you played. Perhaps you see that you are running an old tape that shames you for not being a better caregiver or for speaking angry words. You see how you continue to get stuck. And you can evaluate these unspoken narratives for the truths or distortions they hold.

You now have an opportunity to shape a new, more compassionate (and likely more accurate) story, which may even change the way you see yourself and allow you to make sense of pain and suffering. This experience—thinking, feeling, reflecting, writing, editing, shaping, rewriting—just may contribute to putting your mind more at ease.

Maybe you'll write a messy first draft that you keep to yourself or toss out, or perhaps you'll write a polished piece that you share with the world. Maybe your writing will help you resolve difficult feelings or finish an unfinished conversation. Maybe you'll laugh out loud, or come to see that you aren't alone, that what you've experienced is part of the human condition, that we're all in this together. We love. We lose. We grieve. We go on. Sometimes we even experience gratitude, redemption, and joy.

For now, come just as you are! Start simple, or if you prefer, start big. What comes to your mind?

MEDITATION

Sit quietly for a few moments and attend to the flow of your breath, in and out. Say slowly, to yourself, the following phrases:

May I write to understand what I think and feel.
May writing help me connect more deeply to myself.
May I find words to hold both my sorrow and my joy.

A Few Suggestions

If you can't think of how to start writing, try using a prompt, such as one of these sentence beginnings. Or think of one that works for you:

- ✿ I remember . . . [5]

- ✿ I am learning to . . .

- ✿ So many things have changed for me . . .

- ✿ I want to tell you about my day today . . .
  (as a letter to someone who is no longer with you)

Try writing for fifteen minutes about an experience that's emotionally difficult and hard to talk about. When you're done, take a moment to reflect on what you've written:

- How and where do you feel stress in your body?
- Is it possible to offer yourself kindness and compassion for your suffering?

Brainstorm a list of people, places, and things you love:

- Choose one to write about, using lots of sensory detail.
- Notice how you feel when you've finished writing.

The Cure

We think we get over things.
We don't get over things.
Or say, we get over the measles,
but not a broken heart.
We need to make that distinction.
The things that become part of our experience
never become less of our experience.
How can I say it?
The way to "get over" a life is to die.
Short of that, you move with it,
let the pain be pain,
not in the hope that it will vanish
but in the faith that it will fit in,
find its place in the shape of things
and be then not any less pain
but true to form.
Because anything natural has an
inherent shape and will flow towards it.

And a life is as natural as a leaf.
That's what we're looking for:
not the end of a thing
but the shape of it.
Wisdom is seeing the shape of your life without
obliterating (getting over) a
single instant of it.

—Albert Huffstickler

Welcoming the Life
That's Yours

A Personal Reflection

*It was a surprising sensation, after that first searing year Kris was gone.
I was staying at a friend's house in Provincetown and biking late at night
down a winding hill at the west end of town. Rounding a corner where
there's almost no light, there was the familiar exhilaration of speed and
warm June air, nothing but wind, sky, and trees around me.
Then a thought slipped in: Be careful, you want to live.*

*Live? Wanting to live? What a concept—was this a slight crack in the pain?
I let the moment wash over me, with the breeze and the moonlight. I was still
miserable without her, my girlfriend gone far too soon at age forty-six, of
cancer. But flashes of light were starting to break up the unbearable darkness.*

–BETH

We breathe, we are alive, and because we love, we feel the
pain of losing. Nearly all of us grieve. It *is* as poet Albert
Huffstickler writes:

We think we get over things.

We don't get over things.

Or say, we get over the measles,

but not a broken heart.

We grieve the loss of a soul mate, the person or people we have held tight. We grieve for neighbors and colleagues, for people behind the numbers and charts in the news, for strangers whose stories we know, even if we have never met. We grieve places that we love that are disappearing or being harmed beyond recognition.

There's even a newish word that speaks of this disorienting experience. The word is *solastalgia*. "As opposed to nostalgia—the melancholia or homesickness experienced by individuals when *separated* from a loved home—solastalgia is the distress that is produced by (negative) environmental change impacting on people while they are directly connected to their home environment."[1] It's the feelings of dis-ease you experience when your home, your culture, your way of life, and your very identity are in harm's way. Indigenous people in the Arctic who are losing their sea ice, islanders confronted by rising seas, farmers whose lands are desiccated or flooded already lament these conditions.

We grieve for losses that we haven't yet experienced, but fear will come. We worry that climate disruption is already baked into our weather patterns, that losses of ecosystems and biodiversity, degradation of lands and oceans, are inexorably bearing down on us, threatening the most vulnerable communities first. We hear the early warnings from scientists telling us that humans are creating conditions for new and more-dangerous pandemics.

There is no end run around, or end point, to grieving. And yet, perhaps you can begin to imagine a moment when grief lifts *just enough* so that you sense something changing. You see that some old habits and behaviors don't sustain you anymore and will not support the well-being of our children and future generations. In this clear awareness, you recognize that now you have the chance to make different, more life-affirming choices. You don't have to succumb to despair.

You catch a glimmer of something fresh. Perhaps, it's a feeling akin to hope, a more sanguine or buoyant energy than you have known in a long while. Or maybe, it's a whiff of persistence, of your own grit and resilience. You *can* keep going. You do have resources and inner strength. You can cultivate an unshakeable core.

Even though you would not have chosen *all* of the life you have, you feel some sense of purpose. You feel more balanced, more at home, stronger, and more accepting of what has happened and the way your life is unfolding.

How is this possible? When everything is uncertain, when you still suffer from unspeakable losses, how can there be light? *And yet*, for many people, there is! Some speak of grace or mercy. Others, who don't believe in a higher power, find solace in the human capacity to suffer and cry, but also to laugh, and even in the most tragic situations, to glimpse joy.

What if we got in touch with our vastness, our capacity like a lake or the sky to hold whatever arises? What if we *allowed* everything that has happened, accepted all the experiences we've had, those that we like, those we don't choose? What if we were to pause and allow grief to wash over us and change us (as it inevitably does), and let ourselves open—and be fully here—in the only life that's ours to live?

As weeks and months go by following a tragedy or major loss, imagine that you keep looking inward, trying to make sense of what has happened, trying to see the shape of your experience and how it changes and creates new meaning in your life. Imagine offering yourself great kindness and compassion. Imagine reaching out to other people and feeling fragile new connections.

Instead of hoping for specific future outcomes that may or may not occur, you focus on what researcher and author Kaethe Weingarten calls "reasonable hope," anchored right here in the present moment.[2]

You accept that you cannot know the road ahead. Awkwardly, you try something, fail, and brush yourself off. You adopt the old adage about faking it until you make it. You open to the possibility of serendipity. Slowly, with uncertainty, you begin to welcome it all and cultivate what's yours and yours alone, to grow.

Maybe you discover new passions and interests. You decide to sign up for a yoga class or cooking class, even if it is only offered online. Or, if it's possible, you accept an invitation for dinner with new friends, or you spend wonderful afternoons with a grandchild, rekindle old relationships, or sign up for your summer camp reunion. You go for a walk by the ocean and feel at peace. You act generously, find moments to be of service, and discover that you feel happier and more connected.

Before, when grief was recent, the walls of your home, the ceilings, furniture, floors, everything seemed dull and colorless. But now, imagine that the rooms seem brighter and welcoming. In a corner, one soft gray chair remains for you to visit whenever you feel blue.

You realize that you don't have to leave behind the one(s) you love, miss, and grieve. You *do* go on. You make new relationships and forge new memories. Maybe you even love again. Dusting off your precious photographs, you feel confident that you can always invite the people and beings most important to you to come along, too. Grief is a little more translucent somehow, no longer crowding the foreground of your mind and heart.

What have you learned from your suffering and pain? What do you have to share? How will you spend your precious life, this moment, these twenty-four hours?

MEDITATION

Sit quietly for a few moments, noticing the feeling and flow of your breath, in and out. Say slowly, to yourself, the following phrases:

May I find the courage to bear my sorrow.
May I hold reasonable hope.
May I welcome the life that is mine, and mine alone.

part two

Questions People Ask about Grief

Questions People Ask about Grief

In twenty years of leading bereavement groups, I have listened to people struggling with immense losses. I've sat with them and searched for answers to the questions they asked, answers that might, in whatever modest ways, help them be with and endure grief. Their concerns, which many people who are grieving hold, motivated us to write this book.

How long does grief typically last?

There's no simple answer for this question that so many people ask. For some, grief feels most overwhelming in the first year. Others say they were so preoccupied with tasks, such as planning a memorial service or closing an estate, that they didn't have time or space to grieve fully until the second year.

Though it's impossible to say when this happens, most people *do* experience a lifting of grief's intense emotions as they develop more capacity to bear sorrow, accept what's happened, and find meaningful ways to go forward.

The rawness of their grief begins to change. Intense sadness and a range of other emotions and sensations remain. But many people say their pain feels less acute and no longer blankets everything. Their grief feels softer, more like an ache.

How do I know if I'm grieving or actually depressed?

Grief, characterized by a complicated mix of emotions, including acute sorrow, is a *normal* response to major loss such as death, disease, divorce, or violence in the world. Grief comes and goes in intensity. It is often triggered by a memory, an anniversary, a holiday, or something as simple as a familiar scent. Most people who grieve are still able to experience moments of relief and joy. Their grief does not blanket everything.

There is no simple way to describe depression, but as a generalization you could say that depression has a suck-the-pleasure-out-of-everything quality that permeates all your days.

People who are severely depressed may feel worthless, experience a variety of physical symptoms (such as fatigue, interrupted sleep, and reduced appetite), and have difficulties with daily tasks or activities they used to enjoy. If you're concerned that you are depressed, it's best to find a healthcare professional you can talk to about your feelings and symptoms.

My wife died recently, and I'm dreading the upcoming holidays, birthday, and anniversary. What are some ways I might think about celebrating them?

Many people find holidays stressful, even in normal times. Begin by acknowledging that these first holidays will likely be painful for you. You might wonder whether to celebrate them in the same way as before, do something entirely different, create something that's both new and familiar, or forgo them altogether.

Keep in mind that the days leading up to these occasions might be even more stressful and lonely than the holiday, anniversary, or birthday itself. Try to do some advance planning, so your experience unfolds in the best way possible. Since this will be a time of remembrance for you, plan to make some time to be alone. It's important to acknowledge your grief and not wish your feelings away.

When I'm with family and friends, I feel lonely. There's an empty chair at the table, and yet no one mentions my loved one who has died. Is there anything I can do to make these occasions go a little better?

Some people think they'll upset you if they mention the person who has passed. They believe they're protecting you, though they may actually be managing their own discomfort. They may not understand that you're thinking about your loved one all the time, and that it's actually comforting to you when other people invite you to talk about him.

At a family gathering or an evening with friends, you might try bringing up your loved one. You could say, "My partner would have loved this dinner we're having." Or, "I was thinking today about Joe and how much he enjoyed his garden." Or, you might ask a question, such as, "I wonder what you miss most about Sarah?"

If the people you're with respond positively, be sure to let them know that you feel comforted and appreciate their thoughtfulness.

My adult son suffers from mental illness. He's a wonderful person whom I love, but I miss how he was before the onset of his illness. How do I help friends and relatives understand what I'm going through?

Others don't always understand the challenges you and your adult child are facing. If they're not aware of your suffering, they probably won't know how to come forward and offer the support you need.

If possible, share your feelings with a few friends or family members who are able to offer loving-kindness and compassion to you and your family. You may want to look for a local or online support group for those who share your experience.

Is it normal that I grieved more when my dog died than when my mother died from a stroke?

You're not alone. Many people experience the loss of a pet as a more painful experience than the death of a family member or friend. For many of us, the love we share with animals is simple, pure, and unconditional, whereas our love for another human being reflects the history we have shared together—the good times and the disappointments. For many, love for a parent, a sibling, or a spouse is complex and conflicted.

There are many ways to experience grief, so try not to judge yourself or compare two losses, labeling one as more important than the other. They're simply different.

People suggest that I should keep busy, but I don't have the energy to make plans or go out and do things. Should I push through my resistance, or just stay home?

Grief saps our energy. There's no simple answer as to when it's okay to retreat, or when it's better to make an effort to be with others or plan an activity. It's a matter of trial and error. What's right one day may feel wrong the next. I often hear people say, "I made plans and when the time came, I didn't want to go out. I had to push myself, and in the end I was glad I did."

Try to spend time with those who are sensitive to your feelings, are good listeners, and are able to support you. And if you accept an invitation, give yourself permission to leave early.

My partner died after a long illness. I feel guilty because I'm experiencing more relief than sadness. What if I'm not grieving enough, or grieving at all?

When death is inevitable, it's reasonable to hope the person you love will die peacefully. It's normal and even healthy to allow yourself to feel relief that your loved one is no longer in pain, that the burden of managing their care has been lifted, and that you don't need to spend your days fearing or anticipating death. Over time, you'll have a chance to experience grief's other emotions—sadness, abandonment, loneliness, or anxiety, to name just a few.

If you've been in a challenging or conflicted relationship with a spouse or family member, you may also feel relief when that person dies. Later, you may still experience relief, but you might also connect with other feelings of grief, including anger, regret, and sadness. It's different for each of us.

I've returned to work, but I'm finding it difficult to concentrate on my job. I'm worried that my coworkers are noticing my uneven performance. How can I manage?

Many people share these concerns and experiences as they return to work after a death or loss. You probably *are* underperforming. Because of stress and exhaustion, you may be more forgetful or irritable and have more difficulty multitasking or concentrating.

If your job permits, reduce your workload for a period of time. If you feel safe, tell a sympathetic coworker or manager when you're struggling.

Try to be compassionate with yourself, especially when those around you might not understand what you're going through. It's also important to stay well rested, make time for activities you enjoy, keep your outside life simple, and, if possible, set more modest expectations for your performance.

After my best friend died, lots of people were around. Now, many have disappeared. I still need support and feel abandoned. What should I do?

After a death and a period of supporting those in grief, most people *do* return to their own lives. Asking for help is hard for many of us, but this is a good time to reach out and let your friends, relatives, or neighbors know you still need their company. Unless people have had a significant loss themselves, they might not understand that you're still suffering and still need their support.

You may need to ask a friend, relative, or neighbor to help take out your trash, drop your child off at daycare, pick up groceries, or simply check in on you or stop by for a visit.

Since my daughter's accident, I'm having trouble sleeping. I wake up several times a night and feel exhausted the next day. My doctor has prescribed sleeping pills, but I'm reluctant to take them. What else can I do?

Grief is stressful and can certainly disrupt sleep. It makes sense to weigh the pros and cons of taking medication with your doctor.

The National Sleep Foundation makes a number of recommendations for getting a good night's sleep. They suggest: taking a daily walk, avoiding naps, and going to bed at the same time every night. They also recommend that you turn off screens—TVs, computers, and smartphones—an hour before bedtime.

Some people find it helpful to create a relaxing bedtime ritual, such as putting on fresh pajamas, drinking a cup of herbal tea, reading, writing in a journal, or listening to music. Practicing slow, deep abdominal breathing with a relaxed belly is another way that you can help your body relax before bed.

When I need guidance or I am missing my mother, I talk to her. Though she's been gone for some time, I feel as though I actually hear her voice. Is this normal?

Yes. Some people find it possible to continue to have conversations with their deceased parents or relatives, spouses, or friends. Psychologist and author Lorraine Hedtke works with a practice called Remembering Conversations, which is meant to keep these important relationships alive.[1]

It's natural to wonder what someone you love could, would, or might say to you if she were here. You can remember and invoke her wisdom, strength, and humor. Perhaps you actually hear a loved one's voice, or maybe you just summon a phrase in your mind. Either way, you carry her forward with you as you grieve and go on.

I barely cried when my mother died sixteen years ago, but on the day that would have been her hundredth birthday, I was alone in my car driving by her cemetery. Suddenly I was blindsided by grief and started to sob uncontrollably. How do I understand feelings like these surfacing so many years later?

If you had a difficult relationship with your mother, you might not have been able to grieve right away. If you couldn't accept some of what happened between you or forgive your parent, you might not have had room for sorrow or compassion to come forward.

Consider what was going on for you at the time of your mother's death. Were you preoccupied with other problems? Were any addictive behaviors (such as overwork, binge eating, or excessive exercise) getting in your way and covering up your grief? Reflect on what is different in your life now. What seems to have opened the space for grief to enter?

My friends and family idealized my late husband and remember him in glowing terms. I try to focus on the positive, but he had some difficult qualities, too. Am I betraying my husband if I'm honest with others about the harder parts of our partnership?

Grief becomes more challenging when you idealize or demonize a loved one. There is an expression: "Don't speak ill of the dead." If you literally follow this folk wisdom, you will probably obstruct your grief.

We all have difficult parts. We need to be honest with ourselves about those we've lost and the complexities of being human and loving another.

It is not a betrayal to give yourself permission to remember your husband's strengths *and* weaknesses, or to share with others his fullness and his humanity.

I haven't been able to get pregnant, even though we've been trying for a long time. I don't know how to talk about this sorrow with my friends who are fortunate to have children. How can I begin to share my grief with others?

When you're unable to get pregnant, you probably wonder if your dream of growing or creating a family is possible for you. Because we don't have accepted rituals to acknowledge fertility problems, most people outside your inner circle are likely to be unaware of your struggle.

Try to find a warm, supportive friend or therapist you can talk with about your sorrow. Consider other ways you might bring children into your life, or share your love with others. And remember, this is a time to offer yourself great compassion, kindness, and self-care.

My husband died two years ago. Now, some people are telling me it's time to move on and not keep thinking about him. How do I honor my husband and still move forward?

When people encourage you to wrap up your grieving and move on, they may be expressing their own discomfort with grief and sadness. It can be upsetting to listen to their well-meaning advice.

There's an important distinction in the phrases "moving forward" and "moving on." After any kind of major loss, we do begin to move forward. This is inevitable. But we don't have to "move on," or move away from the person or experiences we've loved. We still grieve. And we can choose to carry our loved ones forward with us with great respect and tenderness.

Perhaps you're comforted by remembering your loved one's humor, by keeping a favorite photo at your bedside, or by wearing your loved one's clothing or jewelry. After your husband's death, it may be healing for you to devote yourself to something that he cared about, for example, starting a foundation, giving to a charity in his memory, or completing an unfinished project.

For the first time since my partner died, I feel some interest in dating. If I explore a new relationship, am I betraying my loved one?

Many people share this concern. It is truly up to you to decide whether exploring a new relationship feels like a betrayal of a deceased spouse or partner.

If you decide to move ahead with someone new, it is important to find opportunities to talk together—respectfully and in non-threatening ways—about the feelings you hold and cherish for the person you deeply loved and grieve. Your new relationship will almost certainly be richer and go forward with more meaning and intimacy if you do.

Since the coronavirus pandemic many people report remembering losses from long ago. Why would these memories be arising now?

Sometimes memories of earlier losses emerge because you were not able to grieve them fully when they occurred. Perhaps you were too busy coping with life. Or maybe you didn't give yourself permission to grieve, or you experienced multiple losses in a short period of time, and you weren't able to grieve them all. Whatever the reasons, losses that we have not processed do return and ask for our attention. A major event such as a pandemic may certainly create an opening for old griefs, as well as new losses, to come roaring in.

Grief can be like a very messy room in our house. It's best to enter slowly and pick up one item at a time. If we try to face and take in the entire room at once, we can become overwhelmed and paralyzed by the magnitude and intensity of our feelings and by all the rich "stuff" that's there.

part three

Deepening Practices

Meditation on the Breath

Most of us are familiar with the concept of practice. As kids, some of us practiced piano, cartwheels, or shooting hoops on the basketball court. Cellists practice, surgeons practice, pilots practice. Here, we describe in detail some of the life-enhancing practices for working with grief that we introduced in earlier chapters.

This basic meditation focuses attention on the breath (inhalations and exhalations) as a way of bringing body and mind together in the present moment. The practice is about being curious about each new breath, maintaining concentration, and feeling the sensations of breathing in and breathing out.

As you attempt to do this seemingly easy practice, you'll soon discover something surprising. Most of us can sustain our attention on our breathing only for a couple of cycles. This is natural. Our minds wander. When thoughts, feelings, or sensations take your attention away from your breathing, be gentle and simply redirect your attention back to your in- and out-breaths.

To get started:

- Find a quiet space and set a timer for five minutes.

- Sit in a comfortable, upright position in a chair or on a meditation cushion.

- You may keep your eyes open, directing your gaze slightly downward and in front of you. Or if you prefer, close your eyes.

- Relax and soften the muscles in your face, then your shoulders, hands, and belly.

- See if you can feel cool air entering your nostrils on the in-breath and warm, moist air exiting on the out-breath.

- Bring your awareness to your abdomen. Soften your belly as you inhale and notice it expanding and opening. On the out-breath, feel your abdominal muscles drawing back toward your spine.

- Notice whether there is a difference in length between your in-breath and out-breath. Try to make your exhalations equal to or longer than your inhalations. This oxygenates and relaxes the body.

- At the end of your practice, draw in three long, deep breaths and exhale fully after each one.

If you experience problems holding your attention on your breath, you may want to try experimenting with a counting technique. For example, with each inhalation of your breath, say quietly to yourself, "In, one." Then, as you exhale, "Out, two." See if you are able to maintain your mindfulness of breathing for four breaths. If your mind wanders or you reach a count of ten, begin counting again, starting at one.

Buddhist teacher Thich Nhat Hanh offers another helpful approach.[1] As you follow each cycle of your breath, repeat one of these phrases:

Example 1: "Breathing in, my breath grows deep. Breathing out, my breath goes slowly."

You may shorten this to "deep" (on the in-breath), "slow" (on the out-breath).

Example 2: "Calming my body, I breathe in. Caring for my body, I breathe out."

You may shorten this to "calming" (on the in-breath), "caring" (on the out-breath).

Example 3: Split one short phrase into two parts: "I am" (on the in-breath), "at peace" (on the out-breath).

As you become more experienced with this practice, try sitting for a longer period of time, perhaps ten or twenty minutes.

Self-Compassion (RAIN)

About fifteen years ago, a group of Buddhist teachers introduced a mindfulness tool for working with intense and challenging emotions, such as shame or blaming. Psychotherapist and author Tara Brach has worked extensively with this practice, which uses the acronym RAIN (Recognize, Allow, Investigate, and Nurture).[1] Here is how to begin:

R: Recognize when you are triggered or dealing with uncomfortable feelings (such as anger, anxiety, or impatience). Without judging yourself, pause, look inward, and acknowledge where you are holding stress in your body. Check whether your breath is shallow and, if you can, relax it. Check if you are holding tension in your body, for example, whether you feel a knot in your stomach, or whether you feel tension in your shoulders.

A: Allow and accept whatever is going on for you. Let your thoughts and emotions be just as they are, without trying to manage or change them, or make them go away.

I: Investigate your interior landscape (feelings, beliefs, and experiences) with as much curiosity and kindness as you can muster. Ask yourself how you are suffering, where you feel sensations in your body, what beliefs you hold about what is happening, and what stories you're telling yourself.

This exploration requires gentle, intimate attention. Brach suggests that you imagine that your child, or some young person you love, has come home in tears after a hard day in school. You naturally embrace the child, offer her kindness, and listen with an open heart to what she has to say. Try to bring this same depth of kindness and listening to your own heart. What does it want to tell you?

N: Nurture yourself with self-compassion. Take time to offer yourself love, kindness, and understanding. If this doesn't seem possible, or you're overwhelmed by difficult emotions, such as guilt or anger, then try to acknowledge these painful feelings and make room for them, too.

As you rest in this awareness of RAIN, notice if you feel lighter and more at ease. The next time something triggers you, try to notice it, pause, and choose a response that is good for you and those around you.

Metta

Metta is a rich practice that calls us to the essential quality of being kind. It asks us to befriend ourselves and all beings. *Metta*, also called loving-kindness, is closely linked with mindfulness practices that draw our attention to seeing clearly and to being in the present moment. In this version of *metta*, sit and repeat a series of blessings silently, first directing these wishes to yourself:

May I be deeply peaceful.
May I be happy and healthy.
May I live with ease.

Next, offer these same wishes to someone who gladdens your heart, someone to whom you readily extend all good wishes for their well-being. As you bring this person to mind, sit quietly and repeat silently to yourself:

May you be deeply peaceful.
May you be happy and healthy.
May you live with ease.

Next, offer feelings of warmth and kindness to a person who is "neutral" to you, someone toward whom you have neither positive nor negative feelings. For example, you might choose a coworker, a neighbor, or the barista where you buy your morning coffee. Silently repeat:

May you be deeply peaceful.
May you be happy and healthy.
May you live with ease.

For many people, this next part of *metta* practice is extremely difficult, or feels out of reach. This next step is to extend loving-kindness to a person you do not like, or find challenging. Don't beat yourself up if this is more than you're able to do. It's good if you can even try to extend kindness, knowing that this is a practice that takes time and effort. Try working with and repeating the same phrases you've been using for those who bring you gladness and for those toward whom you feel neutral. Remember you don't need to be perfect, and you don't want to judge yourself for coming up short. It's the intention that counts.

Conclude by offering *metta* blessings to all living beings, beginning locally and widening the circle to include all humans and sentient beings:

May all beings be deeply peaceful.
May all beings be happy and healthy.
May all beings live with ease.

Getting started:

- 🖋 To practice *metta*, start by becoming aware of your breath. Soften your belly as you inhale, following your breath in. Draw your belly in toward your spine as you follow your breath going out.

- 🖋 Bring to mind the people you choose to include and the *metta* phrases you plan to use.

- 🖋 As you breathe out, silently say the first of the loving-kindness blessings you have chosen. Or say the blessing during both your inhalation and exhalation. For example, say to yourself, "May I" as you breathe in and, "be happy and healthy" as you breathe out.

- 🖋 To close the practice, draw in one or two long, deep breaths and then exhale slowly, letting your awareness return to your surroundings. As you deepen your practice of *metta*, create an intention to bring loving-kindness to all your experiences and relationships throughout the day. Notice when you're behaving ungenerously, or feeling angry or critical, and remind yourself to return home to loving-kindness. Instead of berating yourself, just begin again.

Some people use prayer beads as part of *metta* practice. They make a strand of beads, which they carry in a pocket or wear around their neck or wrist. There's no right or wrong way to do this. Just choose what you find most pleasing. As you touch your beads, bring to mind the qualities of loving-kindness you're cultivating.

Keeping a Gratitude Journal

Keeping a gratitude journal helps to create a habit of noticing positive elements in your life that you may overlook when you focus only on pain and suffering. Doing this counters what researcher Rick Hanson calls "the mind's negativity bias"—the tendency to focus on what's wrong and ignore what's right.[1]

In my writing groups, some people like to use a notebook or spiral-bound book for their gratitude journal. Others prefer using a laptop. Do your words come more freely if you write by hand? Is it easier or harder to express ideas or emotions? Do you feel more engaged than when you're tapping on a keyboard? If you decide to write with pen and paper, take time to reflect on what appeals most to you—blank or lined pages, a fine pen or marker, black ink or a favorite color.

A simple way to start a gratitude journal is to think of a few pleasant experiences you had today. As you recall these moments, linger with them and notice their details and texture, and any images or sensations that arise. This practice is most meaningful when you recall experiences in which someone has been generous or made a difference. If a gift was unexpected (for example, a friend stopped by to visit), all the better! Savor it!

Expressive writing teacher Deborah Ross recommends working with positive statements.[2] For example, if you are pleased that the house was especially quiet throughout the day, you could write in your journal: "I am grateful for the peace that permeated the house today. I was able to think about my loved one without any of the usual distractions." Ross explains that adding a sentence as to why you feel especially grateful for what you have written about can "widen the smile of remembrance." A gratitude expressed in a negative statement like, "I'm grateful that the kids were NOT noisy today" is less effective.

As you become more comfortable reflecting on gratitude, you may choose to write more fully about your experiences—small things you're grateful for today—or about people who are essential in your life, such as your partner, children, or grandchildren.

Writing in a journal or computer file collects your thoughts in one place, so you can look back and see what you were thinking and feeling at different moments. You'll probably be surprised to see your thoughts and feelings change over time (a reminder of impermanence!).

Being with Beauty

Barbara Kingsolver has written about her experience with taking in one beautiful thing every day during heartbreaking times. Inspired by Kingsolver, we introduce a practice of "being with beauty" as a way of cultivating joy and gladdening your heart.[1]

How might you create a new habit of pausing and taking in beauty? In nature or the turning of a season? In art or music? In the faces of children playing? In sports? In a favorite poem or novel? In a bowl made by a local potter, a quilt, or a hand-knit scarf?

Do you dwell in the exquisite architecture of an ant or a butterfly, in the brush strokes and layers of a painting? Can you open your senses so you begin to see or hear differently? Do you feel drawn to writing about your experience? To sketching or photographing? To playing an instrument? To writing lyrics or a song?

Can you allow yourself to be a beginner, to dive in without judging your efforts? As you work with this practice, do you find you're able to carry grief with a little more lightness as you go about your day?

part four

For Inspiration

Poems about Grief

Crooker, Barbara. "Grief."

Hirshfield, Jane. "Hope and Love."

Hoagland, Tony. "The Word."

Kamens, Sylvan, and Rabbi Jack Riemer. "We Remember Them."

Kenyon, Jane. "Let Evening Come."

Kinnell, Galway. "Saint Francis and the Sow."

Kooser, Ted. "Death of a Dog."

Lazard, Naomi. "Walking with Lulu in the Wood."

Levertov, Denise. "For the New Year, 1981" and "Talking to Grief."

Merwin, William. "Separation" and "The Unwritten."

Miranda, Deborah. "Advice from La Llorona."

Morley, Jane. "The Bodies of Grownups."

Nye, Naomi Shihab. "Kindness."

O'Donohue, John. "For Grief."

Oliver, Mary. "In Blackwater Woods," "When I Am among the Trees," and "When Loneliness Comes Stalking."

Réa, Rashani. "The Unbroken."

Rilke, Rainer Maria. "Autumn."

Rumi, Jalāl ad-Dīn Muhammad. "The Guest House."

Wagoner, David. "Lost."

Walcott, Derek. "Love after Love."

Whyte, David. "Everlasting."

Books Worth Sharing

Adams, Kathleen. *Journal to the Self: Twenty-two Paths to Personal Growth* New York: Grand Central Publishing, 1990.

Alexander, Elizabeth. *The Light of the World: A Memoir.* New York: Grand Central Publishing, 2016.

Allen, Benjamin Scott. *Out of the Ashes: Healing in the AfterLoss.* Senssoma Publishing, 2014.

Bauer-Wu, Susan. *Leaves Falling Gently: Living Fully with Serious and Life-Limiting Illness through Mindfulness, Compassion, and Connectedness.* Oakland, CA: New Harbinger Publications, 2011.

Bays, Jan Chozen. *How to Train a Wild Elephant: And Other Adventures in Mindfulness.* Boston: Shambhala Publications, 2011.

Brach, Tara. *True Refuge: Finding Peace and Freedom in Your Own Awakened Heart.* New York: Bantam Books, 2016.

Butler, Katy. *The Art of Dying Well: A Practical Guide to a Good End of Life.* New York: Scribner, 2019.

———. *Knocking on Heaven's Door: The Path to a Better Way of Death.* New York: Scribner, 2014.

Cacciatore, Joanne. *Bearing the Unbearable: Love, Loss, and the Heartbreaking Path of Grief.* Somerville, MA: Wisdom Publications, 2017.

Caldwell, Gail. *Let's Take the Long Way Home: A Memoir of Friendship.* New York: Random House, 2010.

Dalai Lama XIV, and Desmond Tutu. *The Book of Joy: Lasting Happiness in a Changing World*. New York: Avery, 2016.

Devine, Megan. *It's OK That You're Not OK: Meeting Grief and Loss in a Culture That Doesn't Understand*. Boulder, CO: Sounds True, 2017.

Didion, Joan. *The Year of Magical Thinking*. New York: Vintage, 2007.

Ellison, Koshin Paley, and Matt Weingast (eds.). *Awake at the Bedside: Contemplative Teachings on Palliative and End-of-Life Care*. Somerville, MA: Wisdom Publications, 2016.

Emmons, Robert. *Thanks! How Practicing Gratitude Can Make You Happier*. New York: Mariner Books, 2008.

Forbes, Sukey. *The Angel in My Pocket: A Story of Love, Loss, and Life after Death*. New York: Penguin Books, 2014.

Gilbert, Elizabeth. *Big Magic: Creative Living beyond Fear*. New York: Riverhead Books, 2016.

Gottlieb, Lori. *Maybe You Should Talk to Someone: A Therapist, Her Therapist, and Our Lives Revealed*. Boston: Houghton Mifflin Harcourt, 2019.

Grollman, Earl. *Living When a Loved One Has Died*. New York: Beacon Press, 1995.

Hanson, Rick. *Neurodharma: New Science, Ancient Wisdom, and Seven Practices of the Highest Happiness*. New York: Harmony Books, 2020.

Hedtke, Lorraine. *Bereavement Support Groups: Breathing Life into Stories of the Dead*. Chagrin Falls, OH: Taos Institute Publications, 2012.

Hickman, Martha Whitmore. *Healing after Loss: Daily Meditations for Working through Grief.* New York: William Morrow Paperbacks, 1994.

Holzer, Burghild Nina. *A Walk between Heaven and Earth: A Personal Journal on Writing and the Creative Process.* New York: Bell Tower, 1994.

Hood, Ann. *Comfort: A Journey through Grief.* New York: W. W. Norton & Company, 2008.

Housden, Roger. *Dropping the Struggle: Seven Ways to Love the Life You Have.* Novato, CA: New World Library, 2016.

Kabat-Zinn, Jon. *Mindfulness for Beginners: Reclaiming the Present Moment—and Your Life.* Boulder, CO: Sounds True, 2016.

——————————. *Wherever You Go, There You Are: Mindfulness Meditation in Everyday Life.* Boston: Hachette, 2005.

Kessler, David. *Finding Meaning: The Sixth Stage of Grief.* New York: Scribner, 2019.

Kleon, Austin. *Steal Like an Artist: 10 Things Nobody Told You about Being Creative.* New York: Workman Publishing Company, 2012.

Korpi, Sid. *Good Grief: Finding Peace after Pet Loss: Personal and Professional Insights on the Animal Lover's Unique Grieving Process.* Minneapolis: Healy House Books, 2009.

Lamott, Anne. *Stitches: A Handbook on Meaning, Hope, and Repair.* New York: Riverhead Books, 2013.

Levine, Stephen. *Unattended Sorrow: Recovering from Loss and Reviving the Heart.* Emmaus, PA: Rodale, 2005.

Lewis, C. S. *A Grief Observed*. New York: HarperOne, 2001.

MacIver, Roderick (ed.). *Meditations on Nature, Meditations on Silence*. Williston, VT: Heron Dance Press & Art Studio, 2006.

Miller, B. J., and Shoshana Berger. *A Beginner's Guide to the End: Practical Advice for Living Life and Facing Death*. New York: Simon & Schuster, 2019.

Moore, Kathleen Dean. *Wild Comfort: The Solace of Nature*. Boston: Trumpeter Books, 2010.

Nhat Hanh, Thich. *The Blooming of a Lotus: Guided Meditation for Achieving the Miracle of Mindfulnes*. Boston: Beacon Press, 2009.

O'Donohue, John. *To Bless the Space between Us: A Book of Blessings*. New York: Doubleday, 2008.

Réa, Rashani, and Francis Weller. *The Threshold between Loss and Revelation*. North Charleston, CA: CreateSpace Independent Publishing Platform, 2017.

Richardson, Jan. *The Cure for Sorrow: A Book of Blessings for Times of Grief*. Orlando: Wanton Gospeller Press, 2016.

Salzberg, Sharon. *Lovingkindness: The Revolutionary Art of Happiness*. Boston: Shambhala Publications, 2002.

Schneider, Pat. *Writing Alone and with Others*. New York: Oxford University Press, 2003.

Stang, Heather. *Mindfulness and Grief: With Guided Meditations to Calm Your Mind and Restore Your Spirit*. New York: CICO, 2018.

Thompson, Barbara E., and Robert A. Neimeyer (eds.). *Grief and the Expressive Arts: Practices for Creating Meaning*. New York: Routledge, 2014.

Warner, Jan. *Grief Day by Day: Simple Practices and Daily Guidance for Living with Loss*. Emeryville, CA: Althea Press, 2018.

Weller, Francis. *The Wild Edge of Sorrow: Rituals of Renewal and the Sacred Work of Grief*. Berkeley: North Atlantic, 2015.

Willis, Claire B. *Lasting Words: A Guide to Finding Meaning toward the Close of Life*. Brattleboro, VT: Green Writers Press, 2014.

Wolfelt, Alan D. *Understanding Your Suicide Grief: Ten Essential Touch-stones for Finding Hope and Healing Your Heart*. Fort Collins, Companion Press, 2009.

Young, Kevin. (ed.). *The Art of Losing: Poems of Grief and Healing*. New York: Bloomsbury Press, 2010.

Online Resources

MEETING GRIEF AS A COMPANION

Articles at The Creative Grief Studio. *The Creative Grief Studio, creativegriefstudio.com.* Accessed on June 24, 2020.

Joan Wickersham, author. "Grief doesn't have a timeline." *Boston Globe, www.bostonglobe.com.* Accessed on June 24, 2020.

"Resources for Grief Blog," *Resources for Grief™, resourcesforgrief.com.* Accessed on June 24, 2020.

Spirituality and Practice, a Resource for Spiritual Journeys. *www.spiritualityandpractice.com.* Accessed on October 25, 2021.

Turnbull, Joanne, and Claire Willis, authors. "Learning to Accept Grief," *www.spiritualityandpractice.com.* Accessed March 1, 2021.

Weeks, Linton, author. "Deep Grief: Creating Meaning from Mourning." National Public Radio, February 9, 2010, *www.npr.org.* Accessed on June 24, 2020.

What's Your Grief? whatsyourgrief.com. Accessed on June 24, 2020.

BEGINNING WITH KINDNESS

Wolfelt, Alan. "Be Kind to Yourself: Nurturing Yourself When You Are Grieving." *Batesville, batesville.com/be-kind-to-yourself.* Accessed on June 24, 2020.

Wolfelt, Alan, author. "Embracing the Sadness of Grief." *Center for Loss, www.centerforloss.com.* Accessed on June 24, 2020.

FEELING GRATEFUL

Bergeisen, Michael, author. "The Neuroscience of Happiness," *Greater Good Magazine,* September 22, 2010, *greatergood.berkeley.edu.* Accessed on June 24, 2020.

Emmons, Robert, author (multiple articles). *Greater Good Magazine,* multiple dates, *greatergood.berkeley.edu.* Accessed on June 24, 2020.

"In Praise of Gratitude," *Harvard Health Publishing,* November 2011, *www.health.harvard.edu.* Accessed on June 24, 2020.

Marsh, Jason, author. "Tips for Keeping a Gratitude Journal," *Greater Good Magazine,* November 17, 2011, *greatergood.berkeley.edu.* Accessed on June 24, 2020.

"Rick Hanson on the Neuroscience of Happiness." *Greater Good Magazine,* September 23, 2010, *greatergood.berkeley.edu.* Accessed on June 24, 2020.

OPENING TO MINDFULNESS AND MEDITATION

Brach, Tara, author, et al. "New to Meditation," *Tara Brach,* n.d., *www.tarabrach.com.* Accessed on June 24, 2020.

Brach, Tara, author. "Working with Difficulties: The Blessings of RAIN," *Tara Brach*, n.d., *www.tarabrach.com*. Accessed on June 24, 2020.

"Seeking Order in the Aftermath of Loss," *What's Your Grief?*, March 28, 2017, *whatsyourgrief.com*. Accessed on June 24, 2020.

RESTORING IN NATURE

Clay, Rebecca A., author. "Green Is Good for You," *American Psychological Association*, April 2001, Vol. 32, No. 4, *www.apa.org*. Accessed on June 24, 2020.

Grover, Sami, author. "How Nature Can Help Us Heal from Grief," *Mother Nature Network*, April 16, 2013, *www.mnn.com*. Accessed on June 24, 2020.

Louv, Richard, author. "Imagine a Newer World: Especially in these times, we need the courage of our idealism," *Richard Louv*, May 12, 2017, *richardlouv.com*. Accessed on June 24, 2020.

JOINING TOGETHER

Online Grief Support—A Social Community, *www.onlinegriefsupport.com*. Accessed on June 24, 2020.

"Making Grief Friends," *What's Your Grief?*, March 28, 2017, *whatsyourgrief.com*. Accessed on June 24, 2020.

What's Your Grief?, *whatsyourgrief.com*. Accessed on June 24, 2020.

Making Art

The Creative Grief Studio, n.d., *creativegriefstudio.com*. Accessed on June 24, 2020.

Grief and Creativity Blog, n.d., *griefandcreativity.com*. Accessed on June 24, 2020.

"Healing Artwork: Using Art for Healing," *Recover from Grief*, n.d., *www.recover-from-grief.com*. Accessed on June 24, 2020.

Neimeyer, Robert A., and Barbara E. Thompson, authors. "Meaning Making and the Art of Grief Therapy," *ResearchGate*, September 18, 2013, *www.researchgate.net*. Accessed on June 24, 2020.

Writing as a Refuge

Amherst Writers & Artists, n.d., *amherstwriters.org*. Accessed on June 24, 2020.

Center for Journal Therapy, n.d., *journaltherapy.com*. Accessed on June 24, 2020.

Devine, Megan. "Writing as a Refuge," *refugeingrief.com*. Accessed on June 24, 2020.

Murray, Bridget, *Monitor* Staff. "Writing to Heal," *American Psychological Association*, June 2002, Vol. 33, No. 6, *www.apa.org*. Accessed on June 24, 2020.

Oates, Joyce Carol, and Meghan O'Rourke, authors. "Why We Write about Grief," *The New York Times*, February 26, 2011, *www.nytimes.com*. Accessed on June 24, 2020. Subscription required.

Weeks, Linton, author. "Deep Grief: Creating Meaning from Mourning." *NPR*, National Public Radio, February 9, 2010, *www.npr.org*. Accessed on June 24, 2020.

WELCOMING THE LIFE THAT'S YOURS

Lukinson, Sara, author. "The Friendships that Hold Us Safely in Their Keep," *New York Times*, June 23, 2017, *www.nytimes.com*. Accessed on June 24, 2020. Subscription required.

Rosenberg, Liz, author. "After a Loss, Learning to Be Happy Again," *New York Times*, May 19, 2017, *www.nytimes.com*. Accessed on June 24, 2020. Subscription required.

Smolowe, Jill, author. "I Am a Bigamist." *New York Times*, June 6, 2015, *www.nytimes.com*. Accessed on June 24, 2020. Subscription required.

Acknowledgments

This book emerged from my (Claire's) work with people who generously entrusted their grief to me and asked heartfelt and difficult questions, such as "Will my life ever have joy in it again?" *Opening to Grief* is my response to these important questions and my effort to offer solace. I am so moved by each of you who has shared your vulnerability and courage. Thank you.

This book would not have come into being without the help of many people, but two stand out. Marnie and I would like to thank Laurie Skillings and Arnie Kotler. Laurie began copy editing this project four years ago. Her focus, keen eye, and passion for the subject are inspiring and immeasurably helpful. She often dropped everything she was doing when I needed advice or some technical piece of information. Our agent and editor, Arnie Kotler, had faith in *Opening to Grief* as soon as he read an early draft and offered to represent us. His steady presence and graceful and insightful editing brought the book to completion. Working with Arnie is one of the true joys of this project. And to those who shared your writings with us—Beth, Jackie, John, and Debbie—a very special thanks to you.

We both feel continuing gratitude to Peter Turner and the rest of the team at Red Wheel/Weiser who saw the potential in our book and collaborated with us in bringing it forth.

I (Claire) also wish to thank my coauthor, oldest friend, and wordsmith for collaborating with me in writing *Opening to Grief*. It was Marnie's skillful writing, creative ideas, and editing that made this book possible. I also wish to thank my friends and family who accompanied me on this journey and offered support, edits, and invaluable guidance. Most especially, a big thanks to Thalia, who patiently lived through this process alongside me and offered endless encouragement. My teacher, Koshin Paley Ellison, guided me, always with a firm gentleness, in my daily practice from the time this book was born. I wish to thank my mother, Liz, Jeanne, Brita, Marilyn, Otis, Margaret, Catherine, Susan, Joyce, Sarah, Lorraine, Joanne, Alex, MC, Betsy, Bob, Rachael, Carlin, Emily, Olivia, and Eileen.

Marnie would like to especially thank Claire for inviting me into your grief work and this collaboration. In our long and dear friendship, you have supported me through cancer and other challenges; you've taught me yoga; and you have deftly shepherded this project from start to finish.

I would also like to thank my friend Francesca Coltrera for your kind and critical feedback on an early draft of this manuscript. Thank you to Patricia Khoury, my high school English teacher, and to Transom Workshops. You shaped my writing.

Thanks to Shane Hofeldt, my collaborator in making short documentary films. Your rigor and grace in telling stories influenced this book. Thank you to poets (the late) Stanley Kunitz and Genine Lentine. Working with you on *The Wild Braid* was one of my most satisfying projects. I grew and healed in your presence in the garden and in your love of words.

Thank you to my beloved doctors, AnneKathryn Goodman, Michael Seiden, Jessica McCannon, and Rocio Hurtado. I am alive and healthy because of you. And thank you to my acupuncturist Mary Stewart at Berkeley Acupuncture Project for laughter and chats, as valuable and as healing as the needles.

Thank you to my meditation teacher Will Kabat-Zinn who leads with humility, steadiness, insight, generosity, and kindness. You are teaching me how to practice.

And thank you to my daughters, Jamie and Jessye Crawford. Without you, I would not know unconditional love.

Notes

PART ONE

An Invitation

Ellen Bass, "The Thing Is," *Mules of Love* (Rochester, NY: BOA Editions Ltd., 2002).

Meeting Grief as a Companion

David Whyte, "The Well of Grief," *River Flow: New and Selected Poems* (Langley, WA: Many Rivers Press, 2012).

1. Anne Lamott, *Small Victories: Spotting Improbable Moments of Grace* (New York: Riverhead Books, 2014), pp. 29–30.
2. Cath Duncan and Kara Jones, "The Big Book of Grief Rules," part of one of the courses offered by Creative Grief Studio, *creativegriefstudio.com.* Accessed June 1, 2020.
3. Elisabeth Kübler-Ross, MD, *On Death and Dying: What the Dying Have to Teach Doctors, Nurses, Clergy and Their Own Families* (New York: Scribner, 1969).
4. Elisabeth Kübler-Ross, MD, and David Kessler, *On Grief and Grieving: Finding the Meaning of Grief through the Five Stages of Loss* (New York: Scribner, 2005), p. 7.
5. Ibid.
6. Russell Friedman, "The Best Grief Definition You Will Find," *blog.griefrecoverymethod.com.* Accessed June 1, 2020.
7. Francis Weller, *The Wild Edge of Sorrow: Rituals of Renewal and the Sacred Work of Grief* (Berkeley: North Atlantic Books, 2015).

Beginning with Kindness

Naomi Shihab Nye, *Words under the Words: Selected Poems* (Portland, OR: Far Corner Books, 1995).

Feeling Grateful

Barbara Kingsolver, *High Tide in Tucson: Essays from Now or Never* (New York: HarperCollins, 1995), p. 15.

1. Robert A. Emmons, et al. "Counting Blessings versus Burdens: An Experimental Investigation of Gratitude and Subjective Well-Being in Daily Life." *Journal of Personality and Social Psychology* (Feb. 2003): Vol. 84, No. 2, pp. 377–389; Adam M. Grant, et al. "A Little Thanks Goes a Long Way: Explaining Why Gratitude Expressions Motivate Prosocial Behavior," *Journal of Personality and Social Psychology* (June 2010): Vol. 98, No. 6, pp. 946–955; Nathaniel M. Lambert, et al. "Expressing Gratitude to a Partner Leads to More Relationship Maintenance Behavior," *Emotion* (Feb. 2011): Vol. 11, No. 1, pp. 52–60; Randy A. Sansone, et al. "Gratitude and Well Being: The Benefits of Appreciation," *Psychiatry* (Nov. 2010): Vol. 7, No. 11, pp. 18–22; Martin E. P. Seligman, et al. "Empirical Validation of Interventions," *American Psychologist* (July–Aug. 2005): Vol. 60, No. 1, pp. 410–421.

2. Rick Hanson, PhD, *Buddha's Brain: The Practical Neuroscience of Happiness, Love, and Wisdom* (Oakland, CA: New Harbinger, 2009).

3. Rick Hanson, PhD, "Taking in the Good," *Greater Good Science Center at The University of California, Berkeley, Greater Good Magazine*, November 1, 2009, *greatergood.berkeley.edu*. Accessed June 1, 2020.

Opening to Mindfulness and Meditation

David Whyte, *Where Many Rivers Meet* (Langley, WA: Many Rivers Press, 1990).

1. Alan D. Wolfelt, PhD, *Understanding Your Suicide Grief: Ten Essential Touchstones for Finding Hope and Healing Your Heart* (Fort Collins, CO: Companion Press, 2009), p. 23.

2. Jon Kabat-Zinn, PhD, *Full Catastrophe Living: Using the Wisdom of Your Body and Mind to Face Stress, Pain, and Illness* (New York: Bantam Books, 2013).

3. Sharon Salzberg and Jon Kabat-Zinn (foreword), *Lovingkindness: The Revolutionary Art of Happiness* (Boston: Shambhala, 1995).

4. Wolfelt, *Understanding Your Suicide Grief*, p. 173.

Restoring in Nature

Wendell Berry, *New Collected Poems* (Berkeley, CA: Counterpoint Press, 2012).

1. Kathleen Dean Moore, *Wild Comfort: The Solace of Nature* (Boston: Trumpeter Books, 2010), p. ix.

2. E. O. Wilson, *Biophilia* (Cambridge, MA: Harvard University Press, 1984), p. 1.

3. Eike von Lindern, Freddie Lymeus, and Terry Hartig, "The Restorative Environment: A Complementary Concept for Salutogenesis Studies," *National Center for Biotechnology Information*, https://www.ncbi.nlm.nih.gov/books/NBK435817/#_ch19_Sec12_. Accessed on June 1, 2020.

4. Adriana Barton, "Walking Groups Help You through Grief, Step by Step," *The Globe and Mail*, March 6, 2011. www.theglobeandmail.com. Accessed on June 1, 2020.

Joining Together

Robin Chapman, *The Dreamer Who Counted the Dead* (Cincinnati: WordTech Editions, 2007).

1. Henri J. M. Nouwen, *Out of Solitude: Three Meditations on the Christian Life* (Notre Dame, IN: Ave Maria Press, 2004), p. 38.

2. Joan Didion, *The Year of Magical Thinking* (New York: Vintage Books, 2006), p. 37.

3. "One Choir, Many Voices," *Threshold Choir*, thresholdchoir.org. Accessed on June 1, 2020.

Making Art

1. Austin Kleon, *Steal Like an Artist: 10 Things Nobody Told You about Being Creative* (New York: Workman Publishing Company, 2012), p. 27.
2. Mark Matousek, "Felt in Its Fullness: An Interview with Jane Hirshfield," *Tricycle*, April 10, 2015, tricycle.org. Accessed on June 1, 2020.
3. Neil Gaiman, *Make Good Art* (New York: William Morrow, 2013).

Writing as a Refuge

William Stafford, *Crossing Unmarked Snow* (Ann Arbor, MI: University of Michigan Press, 1998).

1. Joan Didion, "Why I Write," *The New York Times*, Dec. 5, 1976, www.nytimes.com. Accessed on June 1, 2020.
2. Stephen J. Lepore and Joshua M. Smyth, PhD, *The Writing Cure: How Expressive Writing Promotes Health and Emotional Well-Being* (Washington, DC: American Psychological Association, 2002).
3. James W. Pennebaker and Janel D. Seagal, "Forming a Story: The Health Benefits of Narrative," *The University of Texas at Austin, Journal of Clinical Psychology*, 55, No. 10 (1999): p. 1244.
4. Ibid., p. 1250.
5. Joe Brainard, *I Remember* (New York: Granary Books, 2001).

Welcoming the Life That's Yours

Albert Huffstickler, *Poetry of Presence: An Anthology of Mindfulness Poems*, edited by Phyllis Cole-Dai and Ruby R Wilson (West Hartford, CT: Grayson Books, 2017).

1. Glenn Albrecht, et al. "Solastalgia: The Distress Caused by Environmental Change," SAGE Journals, *Australasian Psychiatry*, Feb. 1, 2007. pubmed.ncbi.nlm.nih.gov. Accessed on June 1, 2020.
2. Kaethe Weingarten, "Reasonable Hope: Construct, Clinical Applications, and Supports," *Family Process* 49, No. 1 (2010): 525, doi: 10.1111/j.1545-5300.2010.01305.x. www.kean.edu. Accessed on June 1, 2020.

Part Two

1. Lorraine Hedtke, *Bereavement Support Groups: Breathing Life into Stories of the Dead* (Chagrin Falls, OH: The Taos Institute Publications, 2012).

Part Three

Meditation on the Breath

1. Thich Nhat Hanh, *The Blooming of a Lotus:Guided Meditation for Achieving the Miracle of Mindfulness* (Boston: Beacon Press, 2009), p. 18.
2. Tara Brach, "The RAIN of Self Compassion," *Tara Brach*, *www.tarabrach.com*. Accessed on June 1, 2020.
3. Rick Hanson, *Hardwiring Happiness: The New Brain Science of Contentment, Calm, and Confidence* (New York: Harmony Books, 2016), p. 15.
4. Kathleen Adams and Deborah Ross, *Your Brain on Ink: A Workbook on Neuroplasticity and the Journal Ladder* (Lanham, MD: Rowman & Littlefield, 2016), p. 92.
5. Barbara Kingsolver, *High Tide in Tucson: Essays from Now or Never* (New York: HarperCollins, 1995) p. 205.

Permissions

Ellen Bass, "The Thing Is." From *Mules of Love*. Copyright © 2002 by Ellen Bass. Reprinted with the permission of The Permissions Company LLC on behalf of BOA Editions Ltd., *www.boaeditions.org*.

Wendell Berry, "The Peace of Wild Things." From *New Collected Poems*. Reprinted by permission of Counterpoint Press. Copyright © 2012 by Wendell Berry.

Robin Chapman, "Shelter." Previously appeared in *Northeast*, 1988, and *The Dreamer Who Counted the Dead*, WordTech Editions, 2007. Copyright © Robin Chapman. Used by permission of Robin Chapman.

Jane Hirschfield, "Felt in Its Fullness." Excerpt from interview by Mark Matousek in *Tricycle Magazine* April 2015. Used by permission of Mark Matousek.

Albert Huffstickler, "The Cure." From *Poetry of Presence: An Anthology of Mindfulness Poems*. Used by permission of Albert Huffstickler's youngest child, Elisabeth Fraser.

W. S. Merwin, "Place" (excerpt). From *The Rain in the Trees* (Knopf). Copyright © 1988 by W. S. Merwin. PERMISSION TK

Kathleen Dean Moore. Excerpt from the "Introduction" to *Wild Comfort: The Solace of Nature*. Copyright © 2010 by Kathleen Dean Moore. Reprinted by arrangement with The Permissions

DHARMA SPRING publishes books that focus on the practical application of the Buddha's teachings ("Dharma") as a vital source or wellspring of personal, social, and global transformation. Topics include the cultivation of awareness and spiritual insight, working with difficult emotions, mindful relationships, right livelihood, and the environment. Dharma Spring is an imprint of Red Wheel/Weiser. Visit our website at *www.redwheelweiser.com*.

DHARMA SPRING